WITH
LIGHT
STEAM

WITH LIGHT STEAM

A PERSONAL JOURNEY
THROUGH THE RUSSIAN BATHS

Bryon MacWilliams

NIU PRESS / DEKALB, IL

© 2014 by Bryon MacWilliams
Published by the Northern Illinois University Press, DeKalb, Illinois 60115

All Rights Reserved
Design by Shaun Allshouse

Library of Congress Cataloging-in-Publication Data

MacWilliams, Bryon.
With light steam : a personal journey through the Russian baths /
Bryon MacWilliams.
pages cm
Includes bibliographical references.
ISBN 978-0-87580-708-9 (pbk : alk. paper)—
ISBN 978-1-60909-165-1 (electronic)
1. Bathing customs—Russia (Federation) 2. Bathhouses—Russia (Federation)
3. Baths, Russian. 4. Russia (Federation)—Social life and customs. I. Title.
GT2846.R8M34 2014
725'.730947--dc23
2014016274

For Lucille DeView

Contents

Author's Note

The pages that follow are stories, true stories, from diverse places in Russia. Some places I chose because I simply liked their names. Others I selected because I was steered to them—by people, by conversations, by intriguing scraps of news. In each place I did what I have tried to do just about everywhere I have gone in Russia and the former Soviet Union: steam, with others, in banyas. The chapters were reported and researched between 2006 and 2011; prices and news are relevant to the time periods. The chapter titles are responses from Russians I asked to explain, for foreigners, the essence of the banya. All translations are mine unless noted in the bibliography. If I was sure of a quote, I put it in quotation marks. If I was less sure of a quote I paraphrased it, or left it out altogether. No names have been changed.

WITH
LIGHT
STEAM

Prologue

I am naked to the waist, sweeping a fan on a thin pole above the heads, and across the bodies, of about two dozen people sitting three high on wooden bleachers, in bathing suits and flip-flops, in a dimly lit steam room on the outskirts of Philadelphia. With each pass of the fan they shut their eyes against the wave of 192-degree heat and, in its wake, the scent of wormwood, a pungent herb used to make absinthe.

Growing up, none of us would have expected to be here. As Americans, we did not know that such a thing as the banya, or Russian steam bath, even existed. In America, when we hear "bathhouse" we tend to think, "sex."

But the banya is a sexless place—even though Russians steam nude and, across the centuries, men and women steamed together. I learned this in my thirties, after I left the United States for Russia, where I was based for nearly twelve years as a journalist reporting from the territories of the former Soviet Union.

Now I am back home. And I am lost.

I never would have expected this, either—to feel lost at home. No adventure is complete until one returns, after all, and again I am living near those I love most: my grandmom, mom and three younger sisters, as well as rare friends who stayed in touch over the years. I am back even though I know I will need to remake my career ever since American journalism effectively died as a paying profession while I was gone.

I know this language, these faces. I know the sandy soil and scrub pines across the river, in southern New Jersey, where I grew up—its neutral gray skies, its grasping humidity, its everywhere asphalt. I do not mind when people tell me I have an accent, ask me where I am from, and, when I tell them, say, "C'mon, *really?*"

In Russia I was willfully lost—wandering. Here, in America, I am re-rooting. Or so I thought. I did not anticipate the extent to which people had gotten used to living without me, or that the country's credit crisis would migrate from subprime mortgages to investment banks and insurance giants, spawning the recession that has killed off even non-journalism jobs for journalists.

Home is something of an illusion, I know. Like brain scientists say of God: even if he does not exist, we would need to invent him. But the longer I was away, the more nostalgic I became. My American family and friends *were* my country, in a way. Still, how unlikely to have left the stability of 1996 America for the chaos of post-Soviet Russia, then to have left the relative stability of post-Putin Russia for the chaos of 2008 America? How unlikely, too, to be turning to the Russian banya to right myself in an America in which I increasingly feel foreign.

This banya outside Philly was not here when I left. Russian-style spas began to spread across the country while I was away. Now banyas can be found in many U.S. metropolitan areas—from Miami to Los Angeles, from Dallas to Seattle, from Chicago to Boston and, of course, New York. The steam here, in Philadelphia, is not quite as good as my chosen bathhouse in Moscow, but some days it is very good, even exceptional—not just for me, but for the friends and strangers for whom I make steam.

Hurling water into a stove the size of an SUV, splashing aromatic oils onto the wood-paneled walls, sprinkling scented tinctures onto the fabric of the fan, maneuvering the steam over bathers—it is an improbable fate for a guy without any Russian heritage. Not that long ago I was working some twelve hours a day at major U.S. broadsheets on the east and west coasts, looking only to work at bigger, better newspapers.

As a journalist in the States I reported primarily from courthouses, where I developed a hyperawareness of intentional and accidental death: nearly every case I covered served as a reminder that there is no guarantee of tomorrow. Each time I was reminded of this truth I was reminded, too, that I was not living my life as if I believed it was true. Another workaholic day filling the B section of a newspaper with copy was not how I wanted to spend my next to last day.

It was natural for me to observe things from a sort of distance, to spend too much time in my head. But for months I had been feeling, too, as if I were somehow emptying from inside. Twice, even, I had observed myself from above, over southern California streets— as if I were floating, literally, outside myself.

I would never claim to know absolutely the direction of my path in life, but I knew I was no longer on it. It was as if I were climbing the ladder of an outwardly successful career, but the ladder was leaning against the wrong wall.

If I were to die tomorrow, I thought, at least I wanted to be living a more alive life—a life closer to the bone. Such a life, I thought, would mean not only more travel, but living abroad. It would mean learning another language. And it would mean writing things other than news and feature stories—essays, maybe, and short fiction.

After all, I had become a reporter in my early twenties as a test: If I could not do journalism, I thought, I could let go of a need to write that intimidated me and felt more like a burden than a gift. Since then I had shown I could do journalism. It was time to do the other writing.

I decided to quit my job and move to Spain, for Spanish was the only foreign language I sort of spoke, and I already had traveled throughout Central America. Then a friend, another reporter, came to visit me in California. One evening, over good food and much good wine, he convinced me that the destination was less important than simply making a break. He suggested Russia, where he was working, as a first step.

I did not speak Russian, but I had read a good deal of Russian literature in translation. Moreover, I had traveled to the Soviet Union for a couple weeks on a college trip. I did not know anyone in Spain, but I would have a friend, my best friend, in Russia.

When I applied for a Russian visa I paid extra—it was never clear to whom—to be admitted for an entire year on business, even though I did not have a job. When my visa arrived in the mail I gave my editor two weeks' notice. Then I sold and gave away my possessions. I spent a few weeks in South Jersey with my mom, who took in my two house cats before taking me to John F. Kennedy International Airport, where she tearfully put me on a one-way flight to Moscow.

I had planned to scrounge up some kind of work for a year, then move on to another country, where again I would scrounge up some kind of work for a year—to slowly see the world in this fashion. More than a decade later, though, I was still in Russia: without leaving, I had been able to do all that I wanted to do. I had lived abroad, and learned another language. I had traveled far and wide, to more than forty countries. I had written essays, some short fiction. And I had already begun researching and writing this book. This book, it seemed, was the last part.

Recently, while resting between steams at the bathhouse outside Philly, a friend joked that the banya—with the exception, perhaps, of crude oil and software programmers—could become Russia's greatest export to the United States. Then we realized it was not necessarily a joke.

The Banya Is Everything
«Баня—это всё»

My shoulder is beneath my pillow, my forearm is beneath her pillow. I am awake, alert. She is in sleep, deeply. I can tell because I feel the dream she is dreaming, the swell of its heat between her lower back and my stomach.

I breathe slow, intentional breaths to prolong the moment and capture the scent, her scent, from beneath the chestnut hairs piled loosely at her neck. I look past her bare shoulder, past the double-paned windows, toward the still tops of the birch trees reflecting white moonlight in the dark blue of morning.

She could be one of the ones, I think. She could be the last of the ones.

I know it is not for me to question where, and when, people come into my life. But I wonder why Yulia has come into mine when I am on the cusp of going, why we are starting something in the same place I am ending almost everything.

When she walked into the coffeehouse, while she stood in line, after she sat down next to me, at the only free table in the place—I felt sparks. I often feel electricity with women, but rarely sparks. They seemed so unequivocal when they came, as if daring me to doubt something was there, something special.

With Yulia, I do not yet know what that something is. And I do not even guess. For, if living in Russia has taught me anything, it is not to look far beyond the moment.

I got sparks. Now I am risking my heart to find out why.

So far things feel as right as her body, small and calm and certain against mine. I lift my arm from her hip and place it, fold it, on top of hers, as if to reassure her.

She is sleeping. I did so, I realize, to reassure myself.

The alarm clock sounds and I roll over, pick it up, shut it off. I roll back, slowly. I move close, but our bodies no longer quite fit. The heat has gone away, has somehow gotten lost.

Another alarm sounds and I roll over again, reach toward the floor, turn off the alarm on a second clock.

I set two alarms because we fell asleep only a few hours ago, and today is Sunday. Most of Moscow sleeps in on Sundays, but I never do. I rise early to meet friends at a Russian bathhouse, or banya—even when it is dark and icy outdoors, and, indoors, a warm, lithe body is bowed against mine.

I have been living in Moscow more than eleven years. One of the constants in my life has been the inconstancy of my relationships—the departures of friends, and of lovers. Another has been the durability of my Sunday survival ritual.

The *Russkaya banya* rejuvenates me, keeps me healthy. It quiets my mind when I think too much, when I allow myself to feel anxious about having entered my forties without a stable career, a partner, a home. Some days the banya is everything I need to feel good about the world after a week spent reporting on much that is not.

Friends and I have been going to the same bathhouse for several years. We have tried, we think, every other public bathhouse in the Russian capital. Every single one. And while just about everything associated with the banya is subject to argument, this is not: For two hours on Sunday mornings, we luxuriate in the best steam in the city.

Some go to church on Sundays. I go to the banya.

Yulia is about to find that out.

I slip out of bed, bunch the blankets against her to simulate my warmth. I gather my things—soap, shampoo, razor, shaving cream, towel, flip-flops, felt hat, thick woolen mittens, and wooden folding seat. I place them in a rucksack along with opaque vials of oils and jars of seaweed salt and lightly browned mustard powder.

I drop dried leaves of squaw mint into a thermos, fill it with hot water, and swirl in two heaping teaspoons of ginseng root honey from southwestern Siberia.

I dress in full, except for my boots. I return to the bed and kiss Yulia on the cheek, kiss her awake. This is the first time she will be alone in my apartment. I tell her I have left her a set of keys. I tell her to meet me and the guys later, for lunch. Then I go.

The linoleum on the floor of the elevator is wet with urine. I hope one of my neighbors waited too long to walk his dog.

The inside of the main door to my apartment building is swept white with hoarfrost. I shoulder it open. Immediately my eyes begin to water from the cold. I walk across the young ice in a measured shuffle, an inadvertent premonition of old age. In this manner I cross the four-lane street next to my building, step up on the curb, and turn to face the traffic, my arm pointing downward at a forty-five-degree angle.

I do not have time to use public transportation. It would take about ten minutes to walk to the subway, another ten to travel underground, and another ten to walk to the bathhouse. All in all, it would take more than a half hour to travel less than three miles.

A car headed in the opposite direction slows, makes a U-turn, pulls up next to me. The driver partially opens the passenger's side door. I open the door the rest of the way, stick in my head.

One hundred rubles, I tell him in Russian. Subway station Novoslobodskaya.

"Where exactly at Novoslobodskaya?"

The Seleznyovsky Baths.

"One hundred and fifty rubles."

It is only three subway stops, I say.

He turns and faces forward, stares out the windshield.

He will agree, I know. One hundred rubles, about four U.S. dollars, is reasonable. It buys nearly two gallons of gasoline. He is driving a white Zhiguli Model One, a Soviet-era car that should no longer be allowed on the road. He is more desperate than I am: he drove across a double solid line to reach me, an infraction that could cost him either his license for six months, or a bribe of thousands of rubles.

"*Syad'te*," he says, "Sit."

I drop into the front passenger's seat, my rucksack on my lap. The driver turns up the volume on the radio, which is tuned to Radio Shanson, cabaret music.

We drive without speaking. He opens the driver's side window a crack, lights a cigarette.

We pass an ancient Russian Orthodox chapel of crumbling brick. We pass one of the seven apartments I have rented in the city. We pass Butyrskaya Prison, which is set so seamlessly into a block of apartments that passers-by do not notice it, and are not reminded of the thousands who were brought there, and sometimes tortured, before they were delivered, innocent, to a camp somewhere in the Soviet Gulag.

"Remind me where best to turn. Somewhere here, right?"

I tell him. I use enough words that he can detect an accent.

He looks at me with his right eye, asks, "Who are you?"

I say I am "a person of American ethnic affiliation," a self-deprecating reference that, in this context, has a contrary effect: Russians refer to minority peoples from the Caucasus as "persons of Caucasian ethnic affiliation," but never Americans.

He cracks the window, lights another cigarette. "Your Russian isn't bad."

I get lots of practice.

"The Seleznyovsky Baths. I've never been there. They say they're decent."

The best in the city. The steam room in one of the men's sections is, anyway. The rest of the bathhouse is shabby: the owners keep raising the prices, but do not reinvest the profits.

He snorts. Cigarette smoke spills from his nostrils. "What do you expect? Everywhere it's like that in Russia."

On top of that, most attendants are lazy, surly. When I hand over my six hundred rubles, or $25, they seem to wait for me to say thank you.

"Six hundred rubles? That's an expensive pleasure."

But we have been coming here for years. The guy who makes the steam from ten o'clock to twelve o'clock is a wizard in the steam room. His steam is otherworldly.

I add a popular expression: never economize on yourself.

"You're absolutely right," he says. "The banya is holy."

I seem to notice him for the first time. He is slim, with curly light brown hair and a thin nose that is straining to move away from his chin. His eyes are clear, quick. His skin looks healthy for someone who has smoked two Yava Golds by the end of the third song.

He says that he and his friends steam every Friday evening at a banya near his house in the northeast, on the outskirts of the city. He smiles.

Everyone smiles when he begins to talk about the banya. Everyone.

He wants me to know that this is his second car, that he bought it to *bombit'*, or bomb—to rustle up extra cash driving a gypsy cab. Traffic police will not stop a Model One unless the driver commits a gross violation; drivers of old-school Zhigulis tend not to have money to pay bribes.

I ask him the name of his neighborhood banya.

He pauses. It is not actually a banya, he says, but a sauna.

Something falls away between us. He and I both know a sauna is not on the same level as a Russian banya: the saunas popular in the city are like those in gyms, heated by small electric stoves. It is as if someone chose to drive his Zhiguli rather than the Mercedes sedans passing us as we sit, now idling at the curb, outside the bathhouse.

On a fundamental level there is no difference between Russian banyas and saunas as they traditionally were built, and used, in Finland. Both baths have existed for millennia.

The air in a sauna is hotter and drier than the air in a banya, though. The moisture in the air in the banya, a steam that is not visible to the eye, makes the banya feel hotter. The banya is more intense.

But I am not a steam snob. To each his own, I tell him. The most important thing is that we like it.

We both smile. I hand him a hundred ruble note and ask him to join us one Sunday, to bring a friend.

He says he will think about it, drives off.

I buy a bottle of beer at a kiosk on the sidewalk, stuff it into my rucksack. Two friends are already standing outside the bathhouse. A third man, unknown to me, is among them. Their conversation is visible in faint wisps of white against the indifferent light of the morning.

One friend is the American bureau chief in Moscow for a major U.S. daily newspaper. He is wearing a fedora and a scarf knitted by his mother-in-law. He is pale, unshaven. A cigarette juts from between his lips. A cigarette almost always juts from his lips.

Another is an American lawyer who specializes in multibillion-dollar oil deals. He is hatless because his hair is big—wild. He is letting the dark curls grow long enough to be pulled back into a ponytail. So far this has not diminished his standing in the eyes of his clients, who pay him more than the rest of us earn, combined. He has brought a colleague.

We smile, shake hands, step back into a sort of circle. My face feels puffy from too little sleep, and from too much wine. The Bureau Chief's face, too, is puffy—from lack of sleep and, if I know him, too much beer. Then again, perhaps the puffiness may be attributed simply to what he calls the "pasty white bloat" that happens during the long winters in Moscow.

About a block away another friend is walking toward us. He is Russian, a mid-level boss for a U.S. company that manufactures engines of colossal proportions. I cannot clearly see his face, but I know it also is puffy. It always is on Sundays. He works hard and plays hard, harder than any of us. Almost always I can smell vodka in his sweat.

We catch up on personal news as we wait for the others. An Italian numbers man has threatened to come. So have two more Russians, an American, a Finn, and a Brit. We like to go in together, as one. It is nothing we plan. It just happens.

A modest car with red license plates is being parked across the street. A diplomat gets out, an American doing his level best for U.S. agribusiness. His face is not puffy. His hair and clothes and demeanor are reflective of how he lives: clean.

Rank means nothing this morning, though.

For soon we all will be naked in the steam generated by a floor-to-ceiling stove that holds some fourteen tons of cast-iron cylinders aglow in a Mercurochrome red. We will withstand temperatures of some 200 degrees Fahrenheit for as long as feels right before scrambling out of the steam room, and into an icy plunge pool. We will share in the surges of good feeling that come from the yin of the steam, and the yang of the water—sensations that can be likened to endorphin highs from vigorous exercise, feelings a Russian friend calls "wings on my back."

"In the banya all are equal," goes a popular Russian saying.

We instinctively stop talking, stub out cigarette butts, and move toward the main door, beyond which some three dozen Muscovites are undressing, jabbering, laughing, weighing themselves and sitting still, awaiting the call of the wizard.

We shed our coats, carry them one by one into the cloakroom behind a green curtain and black metal bars. Valentina Vasilyevna looks up from her chair at a table next to the window. She is wearing a white linen smock over a blouse and skirt, the hem of which sits higher than the tops of her knee-highs. Her eyeglasses have large, tinted lenses.

"Good morning, good morning," she says as she rises slowly from the chair. She shows me a close-lipped smile.

Valentina Vasilyevna's voice is melodious and of a low register that is somewhat masculine, like the cut of her hair. She delivers her words with the barely perceptible head movements of a screen actor.

She takes our coats, hangs them on hooks, passes us dark blue plastic tags with white numerals.

"Choose a bundle of leafy twigs," she says. "Take birch. The birch today is fluffy, good."

Bundles of leafy twigs are called *veniki* (vYE-ni-ki). They are the most important accoutrement in a banya. They are used to maneuver steam, to massage skin, to treat myriad ailments, and to infuse air with aroma. Birch twigs are the living symbol of the banya. They are far and away the most popular. But *veniki* can be made from the twigs of nearly any tree or bush that is supple, as long as it does not have big thorns or secrete overly sticky substances.

Valentina Vasilyevna recommends birch, but I tell her I would like something more compact, something with more heft.

"Take oak," she says. "If you don't like what you see, open the bag on the floor, find one you like."

Bathers might choose oak to bring on calm, and rowan or stinging nettles to invigorate the body. They might choose one of the softwoods—pine, fir, cedar—for the aroma, and to chase off skin conditions. They might pick eucalyptus to ease congestion by breathing through the slender leaves. They might turn to the sweet-smelling linden to get rid of headaches.

Sometimes bathers will slip fragrant sprigs of currant into a bundle of birch, or oak. Sometimes they will add cuttings of bird cherry, a plant whose soft leaves harbor a powerful antiseptic and smell of freshly-ground almonds.

I do not want to be late for the first steam. I grab a compact oak held together by a knotted twig. I also buy a bunch of wormwood, which I will steep in hot water to make a broth that is hurled into the stove, delivering the scent in infinitesimal droplets.

The others choose birch. Everyone except the Lawyer. He chooses juniper, a rare *venik* because the tree is vanishing from Russia, and most people do not like it: its juvenile needles prick the skin.

Russians traditionally choose juniper to treat rheumatism, and rashes. The Lawyer simply likes the smell. After steaming he takes the bunches home, to his apartment, where they surrender the last of their scent and turn brown, a pile in the foyer.

From the cloakroom we hasten to another barred window where a pretty girl from Georgia—the country, not the state—takes our money. She gives us a receipt, which we carry through a lobby cramped with a black sectional sofa, chrome ashtrays on pedestals, and space-age hair dryers.

The Lawyer says, "Did you see what she was wearing? She's so hot!"

Every week he talks about asking her out, but he never does.

On a chair in the lobby a man sits hunched, cigarette in hand, towel across his shoulders, droplets of sweat over his bald head. On the sofa a Kazakh immigrant sits next to a duffel bag stuffed with batons of cured horse sausage wrapped in newspaper. He is wearing a proletarian cap. He smiles at us. The gold caps over his teeth glimmer.

Past a door the dressing room is crowded with men who are in the process of leaving, and men who are standing nearby, waiting for them to leave. In Russia, such lingering is called standing on someone's soul. It is something the guys and I try not to do, because anyone who knows what it feels like to have steamed knows that the last thing he wants to do is encounter stress.

No changing booths are available, so we split up. Some of us drop our bags onto benches along walls while others take stray places in booths with men whose names we do not know, but whose faces, and bodies, we do. We give our receipts to the surly attendants, check our valuables.

I am still undressing when they come, loud and clear and familiar: the words of the wizard rebound off the vaulted plaster ceilings, off the pink granite walls of the dressing room.

"All desirous, desirous of warming themselves, gather up, gather up!" (*Vse zhelayushy, zhelayushy pogret'sya, podtyagivaemsya, podtyagivaemsya!*)

Naked bodies sweep past me. I put on my white felt Kyrgyz hat, tuck my woolen mittens and wooden seat under an armpit. I pop off the cap of the bottle of beer with an opener that hangs from a string in a changing booth. I push past a heavy wooden door blackened with mildew, push into the washroom. At the far end of the room, near banks of showers, men are funneling past another door, into the steam room. Their arms are close to their sides. They are wearing only hats and flip-flops.

Hats protect the wearer from heat stroke. They also protect the ears, the hair.

"Walk in friendly, walk in friendly," says a man standing off to the side, his skin glistening clear with sweat.

It is the wizard. The areas over his cheekbones, above his eyebrows, are flushed. He drops his head and swipes the sweat from his face with a hand, the fingers arrayed as if holding a basketball. Most of the ring finger is missing.

He looks up, sees me, says, "What are you doing, arriving late? Hurry up, hurry up! The steam is simply mind-blowing—dry, savory, everything a first steam should be."

I smile, hold out my right hand. Hello, I say.

He shakes my hand, says, "I welcome you, Mister." It is an old-fashioned title reserved for gentlemen.

I hand him the open bottle of Zhigulovskoye beer. He chides me for paying twelve rubles and thirty kopecks when, where he lives, it can be found for eleven rubles. Then he removes his tan felt hat and pours some of the beer over his scalp, and some into a dented metal basin nearly overflowing with hot water.

Grisha is a regular guy, but on Sundays he is transfigured. I call him a wizard because the steam he makes works magic on me, on all of us. He is able to strike just the right balance of heat and moisture regardless of the weather, or the number of bathers. It is an ability that lies beyond the realm of science, or habit, an ability that is guided by something arching toward the divine.

Grisha is in his late forties. His hair is close-cropped, brown, streaked with silver. He has a mustache. He walks with flat feet, and a flapping mouth.

"What are you still doing here?" he says, shrugging his head into his shoulders. "You're missing the steam. I already told you, it's mind-blowing."

He knows I am not going anywhere. I have become something of an apprentice over the years. A friend even calls me Grisha Lite.

I set down the mustard powder next to a box holding bottles of oils and extracts. Grisha retrieves a small brown bottle, unscrews the lid, sniffs the contents, and sprinkles the liquid clockwise across the taut fabric of a wand—a thin aluminum pole about five feet long with a hoop at one end. The fabric blooms in tea-colored splotches.

He puts on a pair of gray felt mittens, picks up the wand in one hand. "Let's go."

I open the door of the steam room, walk in first. Grisha always walks in last.

It is quiet. The absence of sound is the most flattering sound possible for the person who makes the steam. It means he has seized everyone's attention, body and soul. Grisha appreciates the silence, but he cannot withstand it.

"How's it up there, up at the top?" he says. He is asking the men on a wooden deck at about shoulder height.

"Good," they say, words overlapping in unintentional chorus.

The steam room is square, roughly the size of a two-car garage with a high ceiling from which three fixtures cast down sixty-watt light. A window of translucent glass bricks sits high in one wall, along the length of which run crude wooden bleachers. The stove is built into another wall; it is painted white and reinforced with steel beams, behind which are stacked cast-iron cylinders heated overnight to between 850 and 1,115 degrees Fahrenheit. In the middle of the room a metal pipe climbs from the floor to the ceiling; a sheet-metal propeller, painted black, is affixed to the top.

Our big-city steam room is designed for many people; propellers are not customary.

I climb wide steps of pink granite to the deck. I duck my head as it passes through the hottest spot in the room, just inches below the ceiling. No one knows how hot it is, for sure: the temperature exceeds the 240-degree maximum on my thermometer.

I unfold my seat on the deck, sit down. I slowly bring my back to rest against the wainscot, horizontal slats darkened by heat, and sweat. I rest my forearms on my knees, let my head fall back.

Grisha was right. This is a perfect first steam. The aim of a first steam is to deeply warm the body—not to shock it into resistance, but to coax it into a sort of willful connivance.

Grisha called the steam savory. Clearly, it is that. It also is something else. Kind.

It seems silly to attribute to steam a quality such as kindness. The first time I heard the word used in a banya was more than a decade ago, in 1997, during a conversation I was having with a book publisher with a fine command of English. We were resting between steams at a coed banya popular among nudists when he told me, "The banya is a kind place. It is exactly what we need more of in Moscow."

I had not lived long in the city, and was only beginning to speak Russian. But the closer I came to know life in this megalopolis of twelve million, the more what he said made sense. Moscow is the most aggressive place I have ever been. By that I do not mean physical aggression; I feel safer here than I do in big cities in the States. (People do not carry guns.) I mean an aggregate of public conduct. Disrespect. Intolerance. Vulgarity. Malice. And, above all, a lack of kindness.

The publisher was right. In the steam room our judgments are tempered by having our physical imperfections open to scrutiny, and the futility of defining ourselves by the trappings of our roles in society.

"In the banya, there are no epaulettes," goes another popular saying.

This steam, the first steam, is gentle. It is generous. It is akin to an embrace, enveloping and unconditional. I could almost fall asleep in this steam. I could, except I feel too alert, too alive.

"Perfect," the Bureau Chief whispers to me.

Grisha is running the wand back and forth above the heads of the men on the wooden bleachers below. They close their eyes. Some smile, others wince as the steam is pushed across their faces, over their shoulders.

Grisha begins to chatter. He speaks in strings of words that tumble forth in round tones, head over heels, down a sure slope to a punch line. Often our group unwittingly plays the straight man.

Today he is referring to us as "the foreign contingent." Other days he calls us "representatives of the Western wing and the New World." It does not matter to him that some of us have been here long enough to become Russified . . . somewhat.

This morning he is riffing on the upcoming visit of the U.S. secretary of state. He calls her Scandaleeza Rice because her words and deeds are often scandalized in the Russian press. I do not listen for long. Instead I close my eyes, breathe in the air through my nose, pull it deeply into my lungs. I relive a moment from last night.

I was lying on my back, in bed, when Yulia draped an arm and a leg over me, nestled her face into the crook of my neck, and began to sniff my skin, manically, like a rabbit. It was spontaneous, sweet. It tickled. Then she laid her head on my chest and ran a contracting hand down my side, and across my stomach. She could not help herself, she said, she just had to squeeze me.

I like to be with Yulia. I just simply like to be—want to be—with her. I am not yet sure how to continue to make that happen after I leave Russia. I am considering steps I have never taken with other girls, girls I have liked a lot, even loved.

I am not against commitment. I just never have wanted the things most people choose to portray commitment. I have never married, never been a parent. Neither has Grisha.

"I'm wary," he once told me. "I'm afraid to take on that responsibility—a wife, a son or daughter. You get married, you answer for others."

Several years ago I lost the biggest love of my life, thus far, because

I would not marry. I do not think I was afraid of answering for her; I was not horribly afraid, anyway. For I still wanted to be with her, and only her. But she wanted more to become a wife, and a mother, than to simply be with me.

Most Russians will say that those who do not have children are not only selfish, but lack a reason for living. Such people, they say, will die alone, and unneeded.

Usually I am granted something of an exemption, though. I am an outsider, after all, a curiosity. Grisha is not. He has yet to marry even though he has lived with five women, the last of whom is his common-law wife of seven years. "One girlfriend used to say, 'Thirty and unmarried is one thing, you haven't sown your wild oats yet. But after forty?' They begin to think there's something abnormal— either with your sexual orientation, or with your psyche."

Russian does not have a word for commitment, as it happens.

Laughter echoes throughout the steam room. I open my eyes.

Grisha has moved from the floor to the deck. He is standing above us, rhythmically sweeping the wand in lulling arcs over our heads. The dry steam feels cottony on my shoulders. Each run of the wand leaves in its wake the aroma of sage, the oil of which he sprinkled over the fabric.

"Thank you," several of us say. "*Spasibo.*"

Grisha usually hands the wand to me at this point. Already he has spent some twenty minutes in the steam room, making steam and fanning bathers. Physicians recommend that bathers limit the first steam to between five and seven minutes, that they steam while lying on their backs with their feet slightly raised, the least stressful position for the body. Over the course of two hours, a bather might spend only thirty-five minutes in the steam room.

But Grisha's magic is strong today. He moves across the deck, stepping with precision among bodies, toward the men lying prone on towels and sheets. One man stands and turns his back to Grisha, who fans him vertically with waves of hot air. An air massage.

"*Spasibo,*" the man says as he sits down.

The men who are lying down turn their faces to the floorboards, straighten their arms along their sides. Grisha stoops over them, sweeps the wand horizontally, to and fro, above their bodies. He squats on his haunches; a few feet lower is a few degrees cooler. The skin over his forehead and shoulders is flushed. Sweat drips from his nose, his elbows.

"Turn over," he says.

The men turn over, lay forearms over their nipples and hands over their genitals. One places his felt hat over his face.

Grisha straightens, puts his shoulders into each run of the wand. His strokes are abbreviated, brusque. Finally, he is tiring.

He turns, exhales from pursed lips and walks down the steps.

Thank-yous drift down from the guys lying on the deck.

Grisha sets aside the wand and opens the stove door, which is heavy and round, like that of a torpedo chamber in a submarine. The hinges sound like a squeegee over wet glass.

"Careful, careful," Grisha says.

Swiftly men begin to leave.

Grisha dips a rusted metal basin into another basin of hot water. One-handed he lifts the rusted basin toward the mouth of the stove, halts his follow-through at the threshold, dashes the water against the scorching hot cylinders. A fleeting splash, then a hiss.

The sound, the hiss, means the steam will be moist, lazy. This is his intention. Moist steam is conspicuous. It is easier to collect and maneuver with the *veniki*. Moist steam amplifies the effects of the massage; the leaves feel hotter on the skin.

Again Grisha tosses a small amount of water into the stove. He gently shuts the door, picks up the wand, and leaves.

The rest of the bathers follow him out, the soles of their flip-flops clopping as they bound down the steps, hastened by a steam that clings to their backs, uncomfortably hot.

I do not. Neither does the Lawyer. I feel good. I decide to stay until the moist steam settles fully from the ceiling to the deck.

Even though we steam as a group, the steaming process ultimately is singular. For we never arrive in the same body. Some weeks we work a lot, others less. Some weeks we are emotionally strong, others battered. Some weeks we travel, we exercise, we sleep well, we eat well, we have sex. Other weeks we do none of those things.

The basics of steaming have not changed for thousands of years, from the Egyptians to the Incas, to the Mayans, to the Aztecs, to the

Greeks, to the Romans, to the Scythians, to the American Indians, to the Turks, to the Japanese, to the Finns, to the citizens of the Soviet Union and, now, the Russian Federation. Every steam in a Russian banya, though, is different.

The biggest variable is us. Today I feel good. I feel as if I need to steam long, hard. So I stay.

The steam room is quiet. Traces of sage, seemingly from nowhere, are reinvigorated by the moist steam.

The Lawyer is sitting near me in a corner, eyes closed, knees up, torso askew. He is bloated. His skin looks unhealthy, and not only because of the lack of sunlight in winter. He has missed three Sundays in a row because he was stewarding an oil deal for which he put in sixteen-hour days, including weekends, before signatures were put to paper.

That is how his life works. He attains a semblance of harmony until a deal comes along, then he disappears for weeks. When we next see him, he looks like this.

He seems to have given himself over to some internal process. He is recuperating before my eyes.

I feel the steam settle first over my nose, then over my forearms. Moist steam always burns where the skin is thin—the space above the eyebrows, the upper eyelids, the earlobes, the nose, the wrists, the knuckles, the tip of the penis.

The door to the steam room opens. Men file in with bunches of *veniki*, glistening wet, in their hands. I reach over, nudge the Lawyer with the outside of a hand. He opens his eyes, rights himself. We rise slowly, duck down the steps.

From the washroom the Lawyer turns toward the pool. I turn for the showers. I am not so hot as to need to cool down earnestly. I can regulate water temperature in a shower, but I cannot in the pool. A sign in red paint, on a wall, says the water in the pool should be 61 degrees Fahrenheit, but it never is—not unless it happens by accident. The attendants merely turn on a tap.

It is well into winter. The water today is 43 degrees.

Cool water runs over my head, my shoulders. It is warm by the time it reaches my feet. I sense that the puffiness around my eyes has gone away. I feel less thick, less dense around the waist. Tension in my lower back, too, has vanished; it was tension I had not known I had.

The phases of hot and cold, the heat of the steam and the cool of the water, are the yin and yang of the Russian banya. One does not happen without the other. Nobody ever has to remind himself to cool down after steaming. It is innate. The body wants it.

The most important thing in the banya is to listen to the body.

The second most important thing is to do what it says.

I make my way to the dressing room, where most in our group have moved into a free booth. I recognize a silver backpack; the Italian Numbers Man has arrived, late, as usual. On a bench next to my waffled indigo towel is a large plastic cup of *kvas*—a dark, foamy, non-alcoholic drink made from fermented rye bread.

The Diplomat left it for me. He knows I like the *kvas* on draft in the cafe. If he gets one for himself, he gets one for somebody else. He is like that.

It is something of a taboo to drink cold drinks between steams. Banya tradition dictates sipping warm or hot drinks, such as my mint tea with honey. Hot drinks keep the temperature of the body on a low heat, continue the slow sweat—that is, continue to make us cooler. Drinking hot tea only seems incongruous, like eating spicy foods in hot climates.

Some of us, though, are drinking cool mineral water bottled on the slopes of the Caucasus Mountains. Others, like the Mid-Level Boss, are drinking beer. Banya tradition forbids alcohol: it dehydrates the body, makes it more likely we will not hear our body's signals, let alone do what they tell us. But lots of men in Russia drink alcohol between steams. The banya is the most Russian thing there is, after all—and nothing can be considered truly Russian if the rules cannot be broken or, at least, bent.

The Bureau Chief and the Diplomat occasionally drink beer, too. So does the Italian Numbers Man on days when he arrives, unshaven, bowed by the responsibilities of a high-paying job for which he is neither unsuited, nor well suited. I do, too, once or twice a year, when I surrender to what the Bureau Chief calls the "pernicious drag" of life in the city.

It is crowded in the booth. There are seven of us, now. I get up, walk into the washroom, smear across my moist skin fingerfuls of the salt extracted from seaweed in the White Sea, in the country's Far North. Instantly it twinges where a cut is healing and in an armpit, where I have a rash.

The door to the steam room is propped open with a broom handle. I go in. Grisha is facing the door, spinning the propeller.

"Look who's come, look who's come—graced us with his presence! Mister!"

He has thrown open the hatch above the glass brick window. Fresh air rushes in from the street as a waving tongue of condensation.

"Here, spin it, please. Ten and ten." Grisha leaves.

I slip my hands into my woolen mittens and grasp the pipe where it is curved into a sort of handle. I spin it fast, ten times in one direction, ten times in the other. One way the propeller pushes stale air down, out the door. The other way it draws in the fresh air from the hatch, draws it upward.

We are trying to return the steam room as much as possible to neutral, to eradicate factors—lingering fragrances, moisture—that could corrupt the steam Grisha is trying to build.

A song continues to repeat itself in my head, "This Is the Right Time" by Lisa Stansfield, the English vocalist. I downloaded it from a disc of pirated mp3s I bought shortly after I met Yulia, added it to the loop on my iPod mini, which long had been monopolized by Tom Waits.

The refrain of the song goes:

> This is the right time,
> to believe in love.

I carry a large whisk broom to the deck and begin to sweep fallen leaves down the steps, into a drum. The wooden boards are wet where men stood, flailing themselves with *veniki*. Stray birch leaves lie flat and wet and dark on the boards. (Someone who will not leave another's side is said "to stick like a banya leaf.") I walk to the stove, open the heavy round door partway; the dry heat will hasten the evaporation of water from the boards.

I would not have dared to do such a thing when I first began coming to Seleznyovka, as the baths are known to regulars. For there is only one person in charge of making the steam in late mornings on Sundays, and no one does anything without his direction, or consent. Grisha has entrusted me, though. It had never been my intention. One day, some years back, I merely volunteered to sweep up fallen leaves in lieu of giving him a tip. As time went by I began to linger in the steam room, to watch how things were done, and simply to hang out and talk, to improve my Russian.

It is unusual for Russians to encounter foreigners steaming knowledgeably in a banya. (False Dmitry, a pretender to the Russian throne, was exposed and executed in 1606 because he never once went to the banya during preparations for his wedding.) Moreover, I am not just any foreigner, I am a citizen of the country that was the enemy for the better part of the last century.

I began to bring in bottles of beer, for the stove. I also began to bring in aromatic oils and tinctures, scents I wanted to experience. Sometimes Grisha asked me to carry in basins of water, and to spin the propeller. Then, one morning, he suggested I use the wand.

I think he meant it as a joke. He could not have known that his proposition was akin to picking first the one who on the school playground was almost always picked last.

I said yes.

I mixed up tempos, angles of the wand. I spent more time than Grisha fanning the guys on the deck. In this way I began to connect with men with whom I had never spoken—men who, as boys, feared an American invasion the way I feared a Soviet invasion. I liked it. And so did the Sunday crowd.

Most Russians would not trust a foreigner with something so Russian. No one I know has heard of, or encountered, a foreigner in Russia so deeply engaged with banya culture.

Still, most of the Russians on Sunday mornings trust me because they trust Grisha, and Grisha trusts me—to a point, anyway.

I feel a brotherhood with Grisha. I consider him a friend. But he does not consider me a friend. He says he has no friends. A true friend, he says, is someone who will come to his aid when the chips are down, who will lend him money unconditionally, who will split a bottle of vodka with him when he is feeling low. Grisha says he wants true friendship, but he trusts no one.

Still, he has invited me to his apartment for holiday dinners. He has introduced me to his relatives, and to his common-law wife, Marina. Not long ago he even invited me to a hotel ballroom for his forty-fifth birthday party—a big deal in a country where the average life span of a man is fifty-eight years.

Grisha is a carpenter by trade, but he has not held a steady job since the automobile factory where he worked, ZIL, was shuttered in 1986. "I had a good salary. Everything was in chocolate. Then perestroika came around, and I became a nobody. I was just a carpenter with a nothing salary."

He did odd jobs here, at the bathhouse, until he fell out with the director, who in the late 1990s was assassinated—gunned down in the cafe where the Diplomat buys *kvas*—under circumstances believed to be related to either an unpaid debt, or an ownership grab. No one was ever charged.

Grisha kept his connections, though, and on Mondays, when the bathhouse is closed for a thorough cleaning, a small group of men gathered to steam privately. Grisha was invited, too, and took turns making the steam.

"I was just bored. It's not interesting for me to just sit there, to just lie there."

It turned out that he had a knack for making steam, and soon gained a reputation. The group asked him to come in, specially, on other days of the week. They made it worth his while. It is an unlikely fate for someone who, until the late 1980s, steamed only once a year—on his birthday, April Fools' Day.

While Grisha is not indifferent to accolades, he ultimately is here for the tips—two hundred rubles, one hundred rubles, even fifty. Most Sundays some three dozen men come for his steam. Grisha does not have much of an ego, but he will allow that "no one goes where the steam is shit."

His full name—his first name and patronymic—is Grigory Aleksandrovich. Few, other than me, know his last name.

He returns to the steam room carrying a basin of hot water. He holds it away from his body, crab-like, so water does not splash

Grisha—an oak *venik* in his left hand—seated on the upper bench at the lowest point of the steam room at the baths at "Seleznyovka." The fan he uses to maneuver steam is at his back. This is his normal get-up: wool felt hat, woolen gloves, and flip-flops. The light is natural, streaming through a small window in the wall (*fortochka*) through which fresh air is introduced while making new steam. Credit: James Hill onto his genitals. He sets down the basin on a pallet at the base of the stove, brings in another, and another. On his way out, he says, "Seven and seven."

I spin the propeller seven times one way, seven times the other.

Why not six times, or eight times? Grisha could not say. "I'm not a theorist, I'm a practitioner. I can hurl water," he once told me. "How do I know how much to toss in? I don't. I do it based on sensations, on feelings, I guess."

He does not eschew theory altogether. "Earlier I used to make the steam a lot weaker, on a level that was comfortable for everyone. I've since come to the conclusion that steam must be more moist than dry."

I am on the last rotation of the propeller when Grisha returns. "Enough," he says.

He walks to the stove, reaches up, opens the door. He scoops a half gallon or so of hot water in a basin and stands upright, his shoulders perpendicular to the stove, the basin resting just off his hip—one hand gripping the rim, the other supporting the underside. The pose speaks to the immutability of the banya: it is identical to that of a man making steam in an etching by Emelyan Korneev from 1812.

Grisha coils his body, then uncoils, his torso pursuing his hips. One hand releases the basin while the other carries it across his body, upward, toward the mouth of the stove. When the basin is within inches of the threshold he snaps it back, empty. The water soars over the cylinders, droplets trailing like the tail of a comet—some turning into steam as they travel. Most of the water splashes against the back of the stove, some ten feet away.

I cannot see what is happening with the water. I know, though, by sound. Water hurled the right way lands with the sound of a wave crashing into a sandy beach. It is not the sound of a wave crashing against rocks. The crash—which is called a clap, or *khlopok*, in Russian—is the sound of the transformation of water into gas, the very creation of steam.

That sound indicates an ideal steam, a light steam.

Grisha waits about ten seconds, scoops up more water, hurls it. Again a wave crashes. Then he dips the basin into a mixture of water and beer, hurls that. Again, a crash. He hurls more pure water,

Grisha hurling water into the stove in the steam room at "Seleznya." The water is drawn from the zinc-plated basins at his feet: two basins are filled with hot tap water, while a third holds hot water infused with lightly browned mustard powder, and strained through a linen bed sheet. The water travels past the threshold of the door—round, and hinged, like that of a torpedo tube in a submarine—then over and against fourteen tons of pig-iron cylinders, turning into steam that bursts out the hatch, invisible, against the tile wall to his right, then dispersing throughout the steam room.

In the lower left of this 1812 engraving by Emelyan Korneev a man is about to hurl water from a small wooden tub into the stove, making steam in the same manner as Grisha does today—some two hundred years later. The image speaks to the immutability of banya culture. At the same time, the work depicts a period in Russian history when men and women steamed together, a rarity in today's public baths. (Coed bathing is explored in depth in the chapter, *The Banya Is an Entire Philosophy*). Credit: Wellcome Images

because steam with too much beer stings the eyes. He pushes shut the stove door, leaves.

Already I can feel the delicate heft of the steam, which carries the aroma of fresh hops, weightless and crumbly. Some liken the smell to that of bread, baking. "With beer, you sense the steam," Grisha told me once. "Such a steam embodies a kind of heaviness, as if you've wrapped yourself up in something."

Beer steam is the Bureau Chief's favorite smell in the world.

I spin the propeller again, seven and seven.

Grisha comes back, repeats the scooping and hurling of water and the beer mixture. Again, he leaves. Again, I spin the propeller.

When he returns he climbs the steps, raises a hand toward the ceiling. "Excellent, excellent," he says. "Very good."

An elderly man comes in, sits low on a bench. It is against banya etiquette to enter a steam room while steam is being made—unless, of course, one is helping to make it.

Grisha hurls in more water, then more water and beer. He closes the stove door, turns. "Three and three." He walks off toward the showers, to cool.

I spin the propeller. Already bathers, anxious, some with hands on the shoulders of school-age sons, are peering in from the entrance of the steam room.

Grisha returns, stops in the middle of the room. He and I look at each other. We know we have nailed it. The steam ensconces us. It is hot, but not scorching. It is euphoric.

"Throw in two. Big ones. I'll go call the guys," Grisha says.

I ask the elderly man if he would like to stay. "No," he says. "I just needed to warm my bones."

I shut the hatch above the glass brick window. Then I shut the door to the steam room, bolt it from the inside: big water makes big steam, and big steam displaces a lot of air—air that would otherwise blow open the door, corrupting the microclimate we have created.

I am a bit nervous. If I do not hurl the water properly our light steam easily could turn into a heavy steam.

The water from my first basin goes far but seems neither to crash, nor sizzle. Steam bursts out the stove door, roils over my shoulder. The water from the second basin lands so well, though, that I wish Grisha were here to hear it.

Creaks. Squeaks. A latch drops into place.

I grab a bottle of beer, cover the hole with a thumb, and shake. I direct a spray of foam clockwise over the stove door, guaranteeing that the aroma will greet each man as he walks through the door, will yank him out of his head and into the moment.

I slide open the bolt of the door, walk out, pull the door tightly behind me. Some two dozen men are massed around the doorway. They part to let me through.

My heart is beating, fast. The skin on my upper arms and the tops of my thighs is a wan red speckled with white blotches, a pattern guys in our group call leopard skin. The blotches are temporary, a sign that the body is struggling to keep cool.

The bathers look toward Grisha, who is standing to the side, a mug of hot tea in a hand. He takes a sip.

About ten seconds pass. Bathers again look to Grisha.

"Walk in, walk in," he says.

I make my way to the pool, walk down the steps into the water, the level of which reaches my neck. I soak for about half a minute. (A bather once told me he comes on Sundays more for the sensations from the cold plunge pool, than the steam room.)

When I return to the washroom, Grisha asks, "Are you going to fan?"

I would prefer to sit low in the steam room, to relax.

Sure, I say, only no orange, no lemon.

"What are you talking about? Lemon is wonderful with beer."

Citrus oils can overwhelm the aroma of the beer, can linger too long in the nostrils. I prefer pine oil with beer. It leaves its mark, yet yields the stage—like I do with Grisha.

You fan, I say, you use the lemon. I fan, we use the pine.

"Whatever you say, Mister. You're the boss here."

We walk into the steam room. It is not only quiet, but utterly still.

Grisha walks swiftly toward the stove, says, "I'm throwing in two more."

"No, no!"

"Don't!"

Grisha is kidding. Two more basins of water would transform the steam, would destroy that which he has so nimbly created.

I run the wand above the heads of the men sitting on the lower benches, on the bleachers. "Soak it up," Grisha says, "it's not every day you get fanned by an intelligence agent of the United States of America!"

Again, laughter. The new faces seem surprised to see an American here, fanning them—more surprised, perhaps, than to learn I am a spy. Any American journalist who has spent considerable time in Russia surely has been outed as a CIA agent. That is the joke. It might seem misplaced, even benign, some twenty years after the end of the Cold War. But the Kremlin line maintains that the United States, the North Atlantic Treaty Organization and its agents—spies cloaked as journalists, businessmen, and employees of non-governmental organizations—are colluding to finally bring Russia to its knees, to gain control over its natural resources and its boundless cache of secrets.

The paranoia is so great that the Federal Security Service, or FSB, the main successor to the KGB, has even been sending agents to spy on us, the foreign contingent—here, in the banya, on Sundays. We know because FSB agents questioned a Russian employee at the Moscow bureau of an American newspaper, referring to us as the "Russia-hating banya group."

I climb the steps, reach the wand toward the ceiling, pull it down, direct the hottest steam over the men on the deck. I make my way to those lying on towels and sheets. I squat on my haunches, loll the wand in the sign of infinity. Then I flip the hoop end nearly parallel to the floor and push the air onto, not across, the row of bare backs.

Roll over, I say.

The men roll over, cover their sensitive parts with hands.

I feel a hint of nausea in my gut. I have been in the steam room for more than a half hour, with a short break to cool in the pool. I also have not eaten this morning; it is best to eat something before steaming, something light.

I move the wand over the chests with more vigor, less tact.

One guy says, "That's enough."

But I do not stop.

I didn't understand you, I say. Sorry, I say, but Russian isn't my native tongue.

Again, laughter.

One man leaps up, races on tiptoes down the stairs and out the door, casting over his shoulder a good-natured, "Sadist!"

"Enough," Grisha says, "you're spoiling them."

Over the remaining hour I help Grisha build two more steams. One delivers an aroma of lightly-browned mustard powder with horserad-ish root, accented by orange-scented oil on the wand. The other steam bears the scent of the wormwood with that of a sweet-smelling herb, garden lovage; the wand is sprinkled with a tincture of mint.

During the final steam, which is especially moist, Grisha pulls a black balaclava over his face, slips his hands into black woolen mit-tens that reach the elbows. The mask and gloves protect the skin from the hot-hot steam. They also make him look like an executioner.

The look seems both to intimidate, and excite, the Lawyer's colleague.

I shave, dress. A post-banya shave is so close that I do not have to shave for two days.

The Diplomat soaks his feet in a basin of warm water while he sits on a granite slab in the washroom, lathering up. He always sits, serene and alone, at the end of a steam.

Each of us leaves as soon as he is fully dressed, so as not to begin to sweat anew in the humid dressing room. We pass the Kazakh selling horse sausage in the lobby, pass another man, ethnic Russian, who is selling smoked fish and caviar poached from the waters of Astrakhan, a port city on the Caspian Sea.

I pick up my coat. Valentina Vasilyevna tells me, "With light steam!" (*S lyogkim parom!*)

It is the phrase used in lieu of goodbye after steaming. It is a wish, a truly warm-hearted wish.

Outside we reconvene in a circle, talk, wait for the others. Our eyes are clear, bright. The skin on our faces is aglow. Even the pasty white bloat has left the Bureau Chief, who is smiling—and not merely because he is smoking his first post-banya cigarette.

One friend, an American, likens the sensations after steaming to the sensations after particularly good sex. An acquaintance, a female Russian skydiver, once put it this way: "The banya is an orgasm!"

I will not go so far as to say we look good, but clearly we all look better. "You don't age on the day you steam in the banya," goes a Russian proverb, which rhymes. (*V tot den' ne starish'sya, kotoryi v bane parish'sya.*)

We walk to a Chinese restaurant down the street. The spices indigenous to the Sichuan province are not tempered for the Russian palate. They induce a second sweat of the day.

It is good to eat after the banya, but not to overeat. All the same, most of us do.

Yulia is nowhere to be seen. I call. She is still in bed. She says she sleeps so soundly at my place, so deeply, that she does not want to get up. She says it is her best sleep, ever.

She arrives toward the end, waves a hand in front of her mouth in a mock cooling of the Kung Pao chicken. She smiles, giggles. Her eyes are alight.

Grisha and the author in the washroom at the Seleznyovsky Baths. Grisha is wearing a traditional felt hat common to Russian banyas, whereas the author is wearing an embroidered felt hat from Kyrgyzstan—common to older men strolling the streets of Bishkek, and not banyas. The Kyrgyz felt is of a higher quality than the rustic Russian felt, and has held up for more than a decade. In the foreground a zinc-plated basin holds a birch *venik*. Credit: James Hill

Mine are, too.

Her sparkle, our sparks, carry us through the ensuing days, weeks, and months. They carry us until the stuff of the heart suddenly drifts away, somehow gets lost, like the heat of her dream. Something so light is no longer enough.

Every relationship I have started here, has ended.

The Russian language breaks things down into three sexes: male, female, and neuter. The banya is feminine, and she, at least, has lasted.

The Banya Is an Entire Philosophy
«Баня—это целая философия»

I unfurl my scarf in two exaggerated loops, stuff it into a pocket of my coat. I palm off my skullcap, stuff it into another pocket. I hang the coat on a hook. I take off my shirt, pull my undershirt up and over, hang them on a hook.

Dank air chills the skin across my shoulders.

I untie my left boot, shuck it. I take off the sock, scrunch it into the boot. I untie my right boot, drop it to the floor, stuff in the sock. I am pulling off my jeans when I feel someone looking at me.

She is staring at me over her right shoulder—her neck long, her spine bowed slightly to accommodate her hands, which are poised at the clasp of her simple black bra.

Her glance is expectant. It says, you first.

I step out of my boxers, yellow lemons on a field of dark blue. I once washed them in hot water. The lemons now resemble limes.

Her glance falls to below my waist, lingers.

At once she lifts her head and looks past me, scanning the high-ceilinged room and the two dozen or so men and women in it, undressing. She unhooks her bra, lets the straps fall to her wrists, shirks them onto the padded bench of the dressing booth.

"I'm not going to take off my panties, okay?"

Whatever makes you comfortable, I tell her. It's probably best to take them off, I add, to wrap a sheet around her waist: if she leaves them on, they will be too wet to wear home.

She leaves them on. She wraps a white linen sheet high around her torso, inches it up to her armpits with thumbs and forefingers.

The sheet is stark against her skin, the tone of which is dusky, almost ashen. She pulls up her long brown hair in two, three motions, slips in a clip. She affixes a white woolen hat over her head, tucks stray hairs beneath a brim that reaches the tops of her ears.

Oksana is twenty-seven, but she looks younger in the hat. It suits her, and I tell her so. Only I do not call her Oksana, but Ksusha, a diminutive of her name.

I put on my hat, pick up my wooden seat and coarse woolen mittens.

Ksush, c'mon.

We walk as if nursing stubbed toes so as not to slip on the slick white tiles that cover the floor, and the walls. We pass through a door, a dim corridor, another door, and into a washroom that is considerably longer than it is wide. We pass shower stalls without curtains, pass banks of crude spigots painted red and blue. We pass rows of knee-level tables, thick slabs of pebbly cement on rusty metal feet upon which rest oils, gels, body-length mats, and basins of steaming hot water. We reach a door, blonde pine speckled black with mildew.

More to the point, we reach the end of a line at the door. Before us about a dozen men and women are standing, nude. Some are talking, laughing. All are waiting.

My body flinches as if a current had run up my spine and out my shoulders. The evening air, cool and surreptitious, is seeping in from small windows built into large windows, the condensation on which reflects silver under the fluorescent overhead light. Instinctively I move deeper into the crowd, into the warmth. Outsides of arms, thighs. A stray breast, soft.

I turn to Ksusha. She smiles with her eyes, makes them big.

A man's voice carries over us, the echoes of his words round and unintelligible. Someone tugs open the door. We begin to move, to shuffle forward as if through the pinched neck of an hourglass. As we near the door we dip a hand in a cloudy tincture in a basin on a pedestal, flick the liquid from our fingers—over our faces, over our chests.

It tingles where the droplets fall onto the skin. Mint.

We cross the threshold into a high room with wainscot on walls stippled by the faint light from three fixtures, bulbs behind cages. We begin to climb wooden steps to a large deck when Oksana grabs my biceps with two hands, pulls me aside.

She leans in, whispers, "I'm scared."

People file past us. A man with hairy arms and a nearly hairless chest. Women wearing the prevailing fashion in pubic couture—completely shaved or a landing strip, cropped close. A man with a large stomach and a combover, also shaved. Down there.

We see piercings on bodies whose faces suggest never-in-a-million-years. We see tattoos on the chests and upper arms of men, and on the lower backs of women. We see rustic felt hats, and bandanas, and keffiyehs, and towels rendered into turbans—anything to protect the head, the body, from overheating.

When people reach the deck they intuitively fold at the waist, slink beneath the lower reaches of the steam that has massed at the ceiling like smog over a city, only invisible.

Everyone sits, sits close, on benches or the wooden decking.

Scraps of conversation. Laughter.

The last person, a man, yanks shut the door. He is tall, lanky, with long white hair and a white beard, well-tended. He is wearing a white felt hat that approximates a bolero. He climbs the steps, leans his long arms and torso over a wooden railing.

"Hello!" he says.

Applause. Cheers of "Hooray! Hooray!"

"Now we are about to open up all the sins that we are going to wash away. Christians. Muslims. Jews. Buddhists. We are going to wash them all clean," he says.

Today is Clean Thursday, or *Chistyi Chetverg*, the Russian Orthodox holiday (also known as Holy Thursday) that commemorates the Last Supper, prior to which Jesus Christ is said to have washed the feet of his apostles. Russians take it literally.

Over the centuries many in Russia have performed ritual ablution on this day, when water is believed to carry away disease while imparting vigor for the coming year. Some, usually women, scoop water from streams (the water cannot be stagnant) at sunrise, then douse themselves before pouring it over their husbands and children. Others, though, wash in a banya.

The holiday does not harbor religious meaning for me. I am here because I like the atmosphere; there are lots of people, lots of happy people. I like, too, the irony of a pagan custom co-opting a religious rite: in a largely Christian society, typically it is the other way around. Also, I promised Oksana. This is her first time. That is not to say this is her first time in a banya. But she has never been to this particular banya, to this kind of banya. Very few Russians have.

It is not common for men and women to steam together, although it used to be. Mixed bathing has been the norm, not the exception, since at least 945, the year of the first known account of a Russian steam bath. Men and women, entire families, steamed together. They continued to do so even though the Russian Orthodox Church forbade mixed bathing, particularly for clergy, in the twelfth century, and condemned the practice as evil in the sixteenth century; and even though the Senate in 1743 ordered police in St. Petersburg to fine men and women who shared the same steam room, and in 1760 outlawed mixed bathing across the Russian empire; and even though Empress Catherine II, or Catherine the Great, in 1782 ordered police to ensure that bathhouses had separate, clearly marked sections for the sexes, and that only women attended to women, and men attended to men.

In fact, it took a police state, the Soviet Union, and a succession of dictators, Vladimir Lenin and Joseph Stalin, to effectively snuff out the practice. Small private bathhouses were torn down in villages, and larger public baths (often unhygienic, impolite, and of an industrial aesthetic) and laundry works (many with delousing chambers) were built. Centuries-old rituals and traditions of folk healing were deposed by official hygienic standards and slogans, such as, "Go to the banya after work!"

Such banyas were satirized in the sadly comedic short stories of Mikhail Zoshchenko.

Until then, though, the banya had been much more than a place to wash. It was no less than the crossroads of the natural and unnatural worlds, the locus of transition in human life.

Women gave birth there. The betrothed washed there the day before their weddings, separately, and the day after, together. Relatives anointed their dead there. It was home to an evil spirit, the *bannik*—a potentially dangerous place and the unrivaled setting for the telling of fortunes, and the casting of spells. A village banya, at midnight, is the most magical place in all of Russia.

This early Soviet poster—reportedly from 1937, and by an unknown artist—encourages comrades to "Go to the banya after work."

Still, the Soviet government could not stop mixed bathing entirely. In far-flung villages, and secretly in cities, some continued to steam together—out of ignorance, or defiance. And when the totalitarian state fell in 1991, its taboos fell away, too. If every death also represents a birth, in this case the collective exhale—the shaking off of Soviet shackles on forms of social behavior—meant a rebirth for mixed bathing.

Yet it barely made it out of its second childhood. The upsurge in mixed bathing began to ebb in 1998, around the time, not coincidentally, when President Boris Yeltsin literally gave his job to Vladimir Putin. The new power had had enough of the unfamiliar air of freedom, and chaos. So had most Russians. I know, because I was there. I have been steaming in mixed baths for a decade. This banya is a remnant of freedom in Russia unlikely to be seen again anytime soon.

But that is not how I explained it to Oksana when I invited her to join me. I just told her that it was fun, that it was something completely different.

"Ooh, I love that sort of thing!" she said. "I like all kinds of experiments!"

So it is that we have found ourselves here, in temperatures of 185 degrees Fahrenheit in a steam room, in Moscow, with about three dozen naked, sweaty people awaiting direction from a tall, lanky, white-haired man who looks a little wild, and more than a little woolly.

"So as not to violate our traditions, where are our newbies, the new people?" he says. "Come here, gorgeous. Come up here. New, beautiful faces have appeared in our club. What's your name?"

"Lena."

"We welcome Lenochka!"

Cheers. Applause.

"Where is our other one? What's your name, comrade?"

"Sasha." A girl, short for Aleksandra.

Again, cheers.

"German burghers, we welcome you!"

Three Germans, guys, are seated on the deck. One of them no longer lives or works in Russia, but goes out of his way to find flights that connect in Moscow so as to steam in this banya.

"We salute you! Thank you!" the man says. "The steam room is about to begin. My apologies if anyone takes offense in the crush [of people]. Today is a holiday. The holiday will be a good one. And so we close our eyes."

Oksana closes her eyes. I do not. I am watching the man above us as he dips a bundle of leafy birch twigs into a basin he cradles in an arm. He removes the bundle, dripping wet, and shakes it with pronounced flicks of the wrist, much in the way a Russian Orthodox priest blesses believers.

Droplets fall over our heads, shoulders. I shut my eyes. The air in the steam room is overcome with the scent of mint and the merest trace of eucalyptus.

"They've brought us good herbs today, fresh."

A second man climbs the steps. He is short, trim. His hands are hidden by gray woolen mittens that reach the elbow. He holds a wooden pole topped with a piece of yellowed felt in the shape of a wing.

"So as not to violate the traditions of our common steam room, no one has abolished them, we all sit up straight, stretch our muscles, crack our joints," says the taller, and woollier, of the two. "We lift our palms, our noses. We elongate our muscles, stretch them out. Now we relax, exhale, drop our hands, shake out our bones. Again we stretch upward and, just for fun, squeeze together our butt cheeks as if we've seated ourselves on a little lemon. We exhale."

Oksana and I cannot sit on our lemons. We are below the deck, standing.

"One more time we stretch out that which has not gotten enough sleep this week, while we were fasting" before Easter, which is in three days.

He stretches, too, makes a sound like chewing on gristle.

"Now we turn on our resonators," he says. "We ready ourselves and, with a sound from our windpipes, in a middle key, we begin."

A long and steady *mmmm* emanates from his throat.

Over the next nineteen seconds, while the steam room is abuzz, someone in the corner is tossing ladles of water into the floor-to-ceiling stove. The water turns into steam that bursts past the hatch and surges above us, then upon us—causing our hearts to beat faster, causing us vigorously to sweat.

"We've ironed out our wrinkles, made them neat and smooth like the butt cheeks of a newborn," says the man, the roots of his white beard darkening from the moisture.

"*Mi-mi-mi-mi-mi . . .*" We repeat the sound after him, with him.

Water splashes against the scorching rocks. Fresh steam, invisible to the eye, rises to the ceiling before it is brought down upon us by the man with the winged fan.

"A big 'Hello!' to the non-smokers. We exhale as if onto a mirror, breathe in again, more deeply, and exhale again, so that . . . the mirrors fog up."

Phlegmy coughs, smokers coughs, echo off the walls.

"Another time. Actively inhale, exhale. And a third time. Inhale, exhale. You can cough it out now."

More coughs.

"We'll beat on the rib cage—clean out our bronchia, trachea—to the sound of *mmmm*." We do this for twelve seconds, rap on our breastbones with closed fists.

"We're working the shoulder area, the neck, the shoulders, the hip joints. When we shirk the shoulders up to the ears, we say, *be*, when we drop them down, we say, *bo*. Try to straighten the spine all the way to the heels, so that the vertebrae take their places."

Over the next fifteen seconds the *be-bo*'s devolve into *he-ho*'s, and *he-bo*'s, and *be-ho*'s.

"Pause."

Over the next minute or so we move our heads up and down, left and right. "We throw some fluff up into the air and buoy it above us, lifting our chins, blowing it higher—*ptu, ptu, hoo, hoo, whooo!*—blowing it toward the ceiling.

"Then we bring it down to Earth with all matter of words, except for curses."

Some groan, others make animal noises. Oksana caws like a crow.

For the next half a minute we make a sound similar to *om*, hold it. Then we inhale curtly to the sound of *ikh*.

"I ask of you now complete and total quiet. I ask of you two or three seconds of utter silence," the man says. "Nice."

The metal door of the stove creaks shut.

"More to come!" he says.

Applause. Yells.

Oksana looks at me with wide eyes, and a close-lipped smile. Her face is rosy. The skin on her upper arms and chest is a tepid sepia.

We walk out of the steam room and into the washroom, where men and women, their bodies pink and slick, plunge into a pool of frigid water and pour basins of cool water over their heads and shoulders.

Oksana says she wants to jump in the pool, too, but she wants to do so less than she wants to keep her body hidden. I point her to the showers.

Cooling off is the yang to the yin of heating up.

I climb a ladder and leap into the icy water. I submerge, dunk my head three times, slowly, as if undergoing a baptism. I always do. I do not know why.

I climb out, slick the water from my skin with my hands. I walk to the dressing room, envelop myself in a large waffled towel, and drop onto a padded bench. My breathing is slightly labored, as if I had just sprinted to catch a bus.

Oksana returns, her hair up, her sheet pulled high. The beauty mark on the left side of her face is more distinct. My attention falls to her shoulders and neck, the neck of a former ballerina. She sits down, reaches for a bottle of mineral water.

I smile to myself. Oksana might like experiments, but, so far, her readiness to fully submit to this sort of experiment mirrors her approach to dating: it is more virtual, than real. For Oksana and I met online. Twice.

Online dating was a new thing in Moscow in the late nineties. It inadvertently served as a kind of screening process for people with higher educations, and good jobs, because they were more likely to have computers with access to the Internet. For a while it was an effectual bridge to the real world, and that was when we met.

Our first date was at a coffeehouse, Delifrance, one of the city's first. Oksana had taken a long lunch from her job as a producer at a state television station. I felt comfortable with her, but I did not feel much in the way of electricity. Shortly thereafter I left the city for a spell of travel, and I did not call her when I came back. She did not call me, either.

Then again, Russian girls almost never, ever, call boys first.

A few years passed. Then we met again, online.

She did not recognize me. Or so she says. I certainly did not recognize her. She had used a pseudonym. And, while I have a good memory for things I see, her photo was of little help: it was taken with a webcam, from the neck down.

Our second date also was at a coffeehouse. She was more casual, confident. She wore her hair down. Again, we were comfortable in each other's company, but neither of us seemed to feel an attraction for the other that was somehow resolute. Still, the odds are not especially high for meeting twice, anonymously, in a city of twelve million. So out of respect for something we are reluctant to chalk up to coincidence, and an inkling of feeling we are unwilling to disregard, we hang out.

We meet for coffee. We go to exhibitions. Sometimes I help her with her English as she prepares to study photography at a university in London. To me, it is not that important what we do, for I simply like to be around Oksana. She is upbeat, and positive, qualities that are at a deficit in a city that courses with an energy that is gray, gritty, and indifferent—except for periods when it is territorial, everpresent in a way I would characterize as jealous of lasting tremors of joy, of seemingly even the smallest concentrations of light.

This energy is indefatigable. One friend, a Russian, envisions herself blocked off by a brick wall in the markets, and in the subway, to fend off people she calls "energetic vampires." I make sure to get out of the city, to travel at least once a month. I also try to frustrate the energy with its inverse—with, well, love. When I feel as if I am succumbing to the energy, I picture myself casting droplets of silvery white light over and onto the heads of people, and into spaces. It is as if I am a conduit for the delivery of concentrations of grace, an act that, to me, is akin to prayer.

I do these things and I go to the banya. On Sundays I steam with friends, all men, and a few evenings a month I steam with more friends, men and women. Occasionally I bring a girlfriend or lover to the coed banya, but carnal love is bestowed fitfully in my life. Mostly I go alone, or with a friend. Friendships, for me—someone who has never married, who is not a parent—are like droplets of silvery white grace delivered intravenously.

Oksana has told me that her feelings for me are more in her head than in her heart. But sometimes we get along so well that the head and the heart seem to be conspiring in whispers.

Like now.

It could be us, but it just as easily could be this place. "In our banya defenses fall away, and you feel absolutely equal, at one, with everyone else," the lanky white-haired man once told me.

His name is Viktor. From our booth I watch as he drifts throughout the dressing room, stopping to pour himself some hibiscus tea, to chat with the people coming and going, and to visit with those seated in booths where small table tops hold thermoses of tea, jars of honey, plates of fresh fruit and slices of lemon.

Slowly he is calling everyone to the steam.

I look at Oksana, tilt my head in the direction of the steam room.

"Let's go," she says.

She rises, puts on her hat, stoops to glance in a mirror.

In the washroom cool air prattles from rusting ducts, causing a draft. Outside the door of the steam room we bunch up, close—to get warm and, possibly, out of kinship.

"Don't pinch," someone says.

Inside the steam room Viktor already is standing on the deck. "We come in, we shut the door. We pass by, we pass by. We press closer to each other, the more the merrier."

Oksana and I stay low, on the floor. All at once she lets the white sheet fall to her hips. I pretend not to notice.

"My friends—everyone here is near and dear—we are filling up our steam room. I ask for a moment of your attention. It's the best to celebrate one's birthday with friends, in a banya. Today is my birthday!"

Applause. Cheers of "*Ura! Ura!*," or "Hooray! Hooray!"

With two thumbs Viktor liberates the cork from a bottle of Soviet Champagne. He places a thumb over the mouth of the bottle, and shakes. Sticky sweetness rains down upon us, eliciting squeals like those of children running under a sprinkler in summer.

He opens up two more bottles, plastic corks ricocheting off the ceiling. He shakes them, too. The champagne surges through the air. He passes down the bottles to us. We take sips, and pass them along to others. He opens up a fourth.

"Is there more champagne? Give it here." A girl's voice.

"It just went past you."

"Where?"

"Over there."

"A birthday with friends, in the banya, is a wonderful holiday," Viktor says. "One more time, congratulate me.

"Hip-hip!"

"Hooray!"

"Hip-hip!"

"Hooray!"

"Thank you!"

Empty bottles, upright, on the floor of a steam room, are not common. It is against banya creed to drink alcohol while steaming, let alone in a steam room.

"That's all. Quiet. End your conversations," Viktor says.

"Breathe deeply, breathe through the nose. Inhale three times. Pause. Exhale three times, through the mouth . . . We exhale with the sound of *aaah*. Everything bad, negative that has built up in the family, taking into account that children answer for the sins of their parents . . . all the heaviness I amassed in my forty-eight years, over my entire life, we gather it up and send it into the cosmos."

Viktor might be forty-eight, but he looks as if he is in his late sixties.

He makes a whining sound akin to an engine of an airplane in ascent. We repeat after him, with him. He makes the sound, *aaah*. We do, too.

For the next eight minutes or so we progress through sounds from the lowest to the highest registers of the musical scale, sounds that he says help us "to clean out not only our bodies, but our souls." We imitate the act of keeping aloft the bud of a pussy willow with one's breath. We imitate the engine of a motorcycle struggling up a trail on a mountain.

These sounds, these successions of words, are not common to Russian. A friend, a native speaker, calls them a bizarre slang that is tantamount to "some kind of raving."

Viktor tells us to imagine ourselves getting off our motorcycles at the peak of the mountain, then looking up, out, and below. We exhale, exhale again. And again.

"Congratulations! Congratulations! Thank you," Viktor says. "The banya will continue until eleven o'clock!"

Again, cheers.

Usually there are three collective steams in an evening. Tonight there will be four.

I am climbing out of the plunge pool when, at the far end of the washroom, I see Oksana. She is standing, nude, her sheet discarded in a damp pile on a cement slab. My grasp of the trends in pubic couture, apparently, is limited: old school is making a comeback.

While Oksana walks to the showers, I walk to the dressing room. Others are returning to the steam room, in their hands wet bunches of leafy birch twigs that they will use to massage themselves, and each other. I wrap a towel around my waist, fish out some rubles from a jeans pocket, and make my way to the downstairs café. On the way I see Viktor standing in the lobby, talking—one hand on the back of a long wooden bench, the other gesticulating with a cigarette, its smoke hovering in lazy switchbacks above a table heavy with vodka, wines, beer, fruit juices, salads, fishes, and meats.

His pose, I suspect, is both instinctual and practiced: he is a former theater director, primarily plays for children. This evening, though, Viktor is a *banshchik*, the person in charge of what happens in the steam room. Both skill sets are in his blood.

When he was five years old he began to steam with his mom and dad, with other kids and their parents, in a banya in the city of Leningrad, now St. Petersburg. They went once a week on the so-called sanitary day, when the bathhouse, the Ilyachyovsky Baths, was closed for a thorough cleansing. The parents had a deal with the director.

"It was secret," Viktor once told me.

When he was older he accompanied his father on trips throughout the Soviet Union. Wherever they went, the father searched for the best local baths—places where the stoves were powerful, places where the regulars understood how to conjure good steam by manipulating the elements of fire, water, and air. As an adult Viktor continued to travel far and wide, to direct plays. Like his father, one of the first things he did in a new city was board a bus, or a trolley, and ask passengers which baths had the best steam. "No matter where we were," he said, "within a week the entire theater company came with me to steam."

I do the same thing when I travel in Russia—only without an entourage. So did Feodor Chaliapin, the legendary operatic bass. In the early 1900s he wrote that "no matter what city I came to, if I had at least one five-kopeck coin in my pocket, I went to the banya and endlessly washed, washed again, rinsed off, steamed, steamed some more, and began the process all over again."

In fact, Viktor traveled, worked, and steamed through the 1980s, when the government embarked on the experiment it called perestroika, a restructuring that was designed to be economic, but would turn political: in 1991 the Communist state collapsed, and so did centralized sources of financing for the arts (and just about everything else).

Offers to stage plays for children barely covered the costs of travel. So, like professionals all over the former Soviet Union, Viktor began to look for work outside his field. He left the theater. He stopped traveling. Something happened, something he will not talk about. It is the reason why he looks old enough to be my grandfather.

"It was just a very hard time," is all he will say.

He did not foresee that the qualities that made him a natural in the theater would be in demand, again, on an unlikely stage. Like actors in search of a director, an audience in Moscow was searching for a new kind of spectacle.

It was not just Moscow, though. Much of the country was being flooded with new things to try, and to buy. Appliances. Clothes. Shoes. Cars. Music. Medicines. Foods. Magazines. Recreational drugs. Pornography. For a while even things that could not be acquired, or sold, were valued: independent political parties, community groups, clubs for hobbyists, self-improvement programs, leadership seminars, psychological training, and magic. For a while there even was something close to true freedom of movement, of association, and of religion.

There was free love, too, and much more of the kind that comes at a price.

"After perestroika everything bloomed in flowing colors—everything was permitted and nothing was prohibited—and that allowed people to better discover themselves, and to understand themselves," a friend from a mixed bath, Sasha, a former men's champion gymnast, once told me. "If, before, everything was taboo for them, now they could do what they liked, and they could not do what they didn't like. Before they didn't like anything, because they didn't even know what it was."

That meant mixed bathing, too. It had been prohibited for so long that it was new to those raised during the age of *Homo Sovieticus*. It sounded racy. It sounded sexually promising. It attracted nudists, swingers, perverts, and the merely curious. It also drew people like Viktor, those who simply liked to steam—together, with friends.

In 1992 he resuscitated the rituals imparted by his parents. One evening a week he rented the women's section at the Usachyovsky Baths, in Moscow, whose popularity peaked in the 1960s when the director piped new and hard-to-find music into the dressing room. This time, Viktor and his friends did not have to steam in secret. Over the next fifteen years, the dynamics of Viktor's banya club would reflect the heave and sway of the country, at large.

"Every time troubled times begin, like in America during the Great Depression, what rises to the surface? Scum floats to the surface," Viktor once told me. "What's in that scum? The criminal crawls to the surface, right? Everybody understands it's impossible to fight with the criminal who crawls to the surface, there would be gunfire. In the meantime, ideals are lost. There is complete freedom. People don't know what to do with themselves. Stability is gone. People who don't fit in, they begin to look elsewhere for some kind of foothold in life. No one understands what's happening, how it will all take shape.

"People begin to seek inspiration from other directions, to somehow express themselves, to try to find themselves. They begin to form in kinds of bunches. Let's say they begin by branching out . . . by beginning to study some esoteric practice, to go to some kind of yoga—there is some kind of fascination, some kind of peculiarity, some kind of protest.

"Mind readers appeared. Sorcerers. Witches. In short, obscurantism . . . How many bordellos have opened here? How many casinos? In Moscow there are more than in all of America."

It was as if one day, he said, people were sitting in their kitchens talking about the exiled writer, Aleksandr Solzhenitsyn, and the next day they were chewing bubble gum, gorging on Snickers, and swilling "the drink of the bourgeois," Pepsi-Cola.

"Everybody ate it up, filled up on it. All of it was in the scum, the froth that bubbled over. People felt free," Viktor said.

"But what is freedom? Nobody knows."

I know what it meant for me.

I arrived in Russia without a return ticket, without a place to live, without a job, without a knowledge of the language, and without any savings other than the twelve one-hundred-dollar bills in my money belt. I also arrived without an aim other than the rather amorphous desire to learn to live more in the moment.

The move seemed potentially life-saving after nearly three years in southern California, where, at times, I literally felt as if I were hovering above my life. I had not known that Russians are hardwired to live for today, and that the times—no one truly knew what tomorrow would bring—would make it easy for someone accustomed to living in his head to live closer to his heart.

Life was amplified. Living was breathless.

I was completely unknown to everybody except one person, a close friend and editor at the city's primary English-language newspaper, *The Moscow Times*. Otherwise I felt anonymous and outside the lines, such as they were: lines everywhere were being redrawn.

So when a reporter told The Editor and me about a banya where women and men steamed together, I was spellbound. I had visions of bacchanalia. These visions were not quite lascivious, but I will allow that they verged on the orgiastic.

The Editor spoke Russian. He called the guy in charge of the mixed bath, the organizer of a fledgling association of nudists. The organizer told him anyone can come as long as he comes as part of a couple, a policy intended to keep out men who simply wanted to stare at naked women.

But we don't have girlfriends, The Editor said. Couldn't we just come as reporters? For purposes of, like, deep background?

Fine, the organizer said. The next steam would be in a few days.

I was excited, but also was nervous, for I was not a man at peace with his body. I almost always have been overweight, if not quite fat—even when I played sports, even when I did triathlons. Moreover, for some twenty years I gained and lost weight prodigiously because I overate compulsively. In fact, I gained more than forty pounds during the first year of my first job at a big daily newspaper. I since had lost much of the weight, but it left stretch marks, red and spidery, above my hips.

I could not yet speak Russian, but, naked, I would be sharing with people the severity of my clashes with myself. I wear some of my scars on the outside.

Then there was the dimension to my biology that was even more likely to stick out. After all, I had been to a banya with other men, but I had never been to a banya with women. What if I felt myself beginning to get an erection? How would I stop it? And, if I could not stop it, how would I hide it?

The Editor did not ask the organizer these questions. There was nowhere for us to turn for answers, in English. There should have been: the Russian steam bath has captivated foreign travelers for more than a thousand years. Yet most eyewitnesses recorded what they saw with a heavy hand of judgment and bias.

There was William Coxe, a naval captain from England who described a communal bath in 1802 as "such a monstrous Scene of beastly Women and indecent men mix'd together naked as our first parents without the least appearance of Shame, as to shock our feelings."

There was Jodocus Crull, a German émigré to England whose 1698 account characterizes the bathhouses as "often so carelessly built, that it is easier to look out of one Room into the other thro the distance of the boards that part them, which they look upon here as a Matter of no great consequence, though either Sex has nothing else to hide their privy Parts but a Handful of Herbs moistened in

Water, which a great many don't think it worth their while to make use of, being not very shy to be seen by Men, when they are going out to cool themselves in cold Water, both Sexes commonly going out and in at one and the same Door to their Bathing-rooms."

There were other accounts, in other languages. Most were recorded during an era from the late eighteenth to early nineteenth centuries, when curiosity about Russia peaked among the powers to the West. "It seemed to some foreigners that there was something sexually obscene, but in actual fact there was nothing obscene. There wasn't any kind of sex . . . Entire families steamed, sat naked, without paying any particular attention to each other," the late Igor Kon, the country's leading scholar on sexuality, and a chief researcher at the Institute of Ethnography and Folklore of the Russian Academy of Sciences, told me.

Even Giovanni Casanova, the legendary Italian seducer of women, found the mixed baths of Moscow in 1774 to be innocent. "There were thirty to forty people there, all of them quite naked," he wrote. "But since no one looks at anyone else, one does not have any feeling of being observed naked."

Then again, some banyas—segregated male bathhouses, at least—were not as desexualized as Russian-language publications wanted readers to believe. There was a strong taboo against discussions about sex through the tsarist era, and an even stronger taboo after 1917. But recent research has shown that in cities in the nineteenth century, male attendants—who were usually part of a so-called *artel'*, or work team—sometimes had sex with male customers for cash tips. The proceeds were pooled, and divvied up.

Ironically, the truest accounts of coed bath culture generated the biggest scandals. These accounts were not written, but drawn. The most notorious is an engraving by Jean-Baptiste Le Prince, who illustrated the 1768 book, *A Journey into Siberia*, which was written by L'Abbe Chappe d'Auteroche, after he was dispatched to Russia by Louis XV, the king of France.

There is no illicit touching in the steam room depicted by Le Prince. There is not even any leering. Perhaps the only suggestive element can be seen in the posture of a young woman, who, in *Bain Public*, slouches against a low bench—her arms carelessly slack, her

This aquatint by Michel-François Damame-Demartrais depicts bathing habits in Russia from the early nineteenth century, when men and women washed and steamed together.

legs partially splayed. Anyone who has steamed, hard, would recognize the posture as one of exhaustion, not seduction. Neverthe-
less, Catherine the Great refuted the book by Chappe d'Auteroche
as "most indecent" in an essay titled *Antidote*, which was published
anonymously.

She was sensitive to how Russia was perceived in the West. (Russian leaders are no less sensitive, today.) Yet perhaps the best antidote to the ethnocentric accounts of foreign travelers would have
been a dose of historical perspective. For, by that time, travelers had
forgotten that, as recently as the sixteenth century, men and women
washed in public baths in much of Europe.

Since then bathing had lost importance in the West primarily because it was believed to make people susceptible to diseases, like
plague, by opening up the pores of the skin. (In the seventeenth
century, James I of England was said to wash only his fingers. Those
in the French court tried to shroud their stench with perfumes;
Louis XIII, the son of Henry IV of France, once said, "I take after
my father, I smell of armpits.") In Russia, however, bathing never
stopped entirely—not during the Soviet Union, or the Civil War
of the early 1900s, or the Russian empire, or early tsardom, or the
incarnations of Muscovy, or the arrival of Christianity, or the Tatar-
Mongol Yoke, or the periods of rule of Kievan Rus and the tribes of
the south, during which Scythian nomads washed after scattering
cannabis seeds over hot rocks stacked in dugouts of animal skins
flung over wooden frames.

"What is the Russian banya? It's an entire philosophy," Viktor
once told me.

"It's not by accident. In its time, in Russia, the banya was everything . . . That is, when all over Europe they were drowning, pardon
me, in feces and shit, in Russia at that time they were washing themselves. Banyas were built for all rhythms of life."

The rhythms of life in Moscow in the late 1990s were both excit-
able and grim. It was during an arc of excitability that one autumn
evening The Editor and I climbed the stairs to the women's section of the city's Astrakhansky Baths. The dressing room was loud,
and crowded. The organizer of the association of nudists sent The
Editor to one booth, and me to another. He introduced me to its

This engraving, *Bain Public*, is among the engravings by Jean-Baptiste Le Prince in the 1768 book *Journey into Siberia* by M. L'Abbe Chappe d'Auteroche—who traveled from Paris to the city of Tobolsk. Catherine the Great, in an anonymous essay, refuted the book as "most indecent." Credit: Center for Retrospective Digitization, Göttingen occupants, two women—one in her early thirties, one in her early forties, both natural blondes.

They smiled, pointed to a free spot on a bench. They were polite. They had been about to walk to the steam room, but instead sat down, to wait, for me.

I tried to be nonchalant as I undressed. I did not turn my back. I decided that, like most of life's problems, I would face them.

The women escorted me—one in front, one in back—into the washroom, which resonated with splashes and the raised voices of those, skin slathered in suds, who were scrubbing and being scrubbed with hemp gloves and stringy handfuls of bast. The women led me past the cold plunge pool and into the steam room, which echoed with the slaps of bundles of wet leafy twigs against wet skin as well as the breathy exhalations of those administering the thwacks, and of those receiving them.

I stole a smile with The Editor, who sat stoop-shouldered on a bench. The only place in the city where I had seen more smiles, on more faces, was at the Old Circus. And they were on the faces of children.

It did not seem to matter to anyone that my body did not live up to the promise of my face. Soon it did not matter to me, either.

My escorts left me on my own. I steamed, hard, and cooled down, hard. I rested in the dressing booth, watched people and their conversations. I understood little, but I saw that the exchanges were lighthearted, brisk. Often they culminated in laughter.

Clearly something else had fallen away with the clothing.

America might call itself the land of the free, I thought, but it was not this free.

It was like Sasha, the former champion gymnast, once told me. "This banya somewhat changed my psyche, because relations between the sexes took on another complexion: All the same, clothes are a potential physical barrier, and when they were gone, the barrier fell, and positive and negative aspects became apparent."

The negative aspects?

"The negative aspects consisted of an awareness that . . . women look better dressed, than undressed."

And the positive aspects?

"The positive aspects consisted of encountering women who looked better nude, than clothed. That created an agreeable mood."

Not that he really cared. Not really.

Sasha, a former rocket scientist as well as a gymnast, is fixated on bodies; even in retirement he maintains a muscular physique that most men have never had, and never will. He comes to the mixed bath primarily for communion—the opportunity to interact with an openness that cannot be found anywhere else, or with anyone else, not even his wife.

"[The mixed bath] helps people free themselves from complexes, especially women. It is easier, after that it is easier for them to meet representatives of the opposite sex. They aren't afraid to appear unattractive, since they already know that they were seen, and it no longer seems frightening to them," Sasha once told me. "These absolutely flabby, forty-something dames, who have far from ideal figures . . . they begin to respect themselves more after that. Before they thought that they had very serious deficiencies, and they had hang-ups as a result. But when those complexes are shown to be no big deal, they begin to relate to themselves more graciously, as if to love themselves more, in other words. And of course it's very pleasant for them, the attention of men, if it doesn't have an aggressive form."

The Editor and I were the only foreigners at a place that was foreign, even, to most Russians. Between us we called it "the nudie banya." We began to go, regularly.

After all, deep background requires a deep commitment.

On birthdays the birthday boy, or girl, treated everyone to food and drinks. On national holidays the organizer brought in a boom box to which some sang, while others, mostly girls, danced. During the summer and winter solstices people brought in paints, which the guys used to paint the bodies of the girls. And vice versa.

The mixed bath was especially good for my Russian. I learned the difference, say, between stockings, *chulki*, and panty hose, *kolgotki*. A tall, statuesque redhead, Inna, even offered to demonstrate the finer distinctions. "If you'd like," she said, rolling on a pair of thigh-highs, "I'll wear stockings for you next week."

I told her, yes, but she never did.

I later learned that Inna worked near my apartment, literally a block away. More than once I invited her over for coffee, but she never accepted. It was too close. She was safer, naked.

The Editor could not say the same for himself—at least not around Inna. Once, when they were in the same dressing booth, he learned the answer to the question neither of us had asked: What would happen if one of us began to get an erection?

It was the first and only time in a banya that he used his towel in a manner for which it was not intended. Shortly thereafter, he stopped going. He had begun to work a lot, too much. He also had a new girlfriend, a Russian who did not like the banya.

At around the same time others stopped going to the nudie banya, too. By the late 1990s the flowing colors that were let loose by perestroika had commingled into a beige of daily routine that was encouraged by the new power, which was not so much a new power but a reassertion of an old power, the security services—initially on their own turf, and then on the less familiar ground of the Kremlin, the Parliament, oil and gas fields, boardrooms, and newsrooms.

The change in atmosphere was visceral. It could be felt on the street like a drop in barometric pressure.

"All of that froth settled, and whatever was in the froth went away, and whatever wasn't, remained," Viktor said. "Slowly, slowly the word, nudism, disappeared from the mixed bath, and there remained a banya club—lovers of the banya. . . . The plank became lower, became more human. People understood that it isn't for the masses, but for the soul."

I have never encountered ritualistic breathing and chanting in any other banya, anywhere. Although words and sounds long have been a part of the banya culture, they are associated more with ritualistic song and incantations of spells in small, private banyas. The rituals tonight are more improvisation than tradition. Such a thing is to be expected, perhaps, from a director of children's theater.

"It's all an outgrowth of the traditions of the Russian banya," Viktor once told me.

"Of course there were sounds. How else would you expect dark powers to leave quietly? Dark powers leave. 'With steam and screams the demon leaves the body.' There used to be that kind of proverb. Dark powers leave the body."

I do not believe in demons, at least not in manifestations other than metaphor. And I do not believe in dark powers so much as I believe in shadows—the parts of ourselves that we do not like to acknowledge, let alone show to others. But if the shadows are the places from which our metaphorical demons spring forth, then in Viktor's banya the demons are our fears.

It was in a mixed bath that I overcame my fear of revealing my body, naked, to others. This evening Oksana, too, has overcome the same fear. I am proud of her, my topless and bottomless Oksana. She has taken to this experiment like she and I took to each other, over time. Again she has bridged the virtual and the real.

After the third collective steam I offer to give Oksana a massage, and she accepts. I sluice a basin of hot water over the slabs of pebbly cement, unroll my lime green mat. I splash hot water over that, too. Oksana lays down on her stomach, her arms at her sides, her head turned. She shuts her eyes.

I rub massage oil into my palms—warm up my hands, warm up the oil. I begin to move my hands over her in the sweeping arrays taught to me at a school of massage in the city. I am certified to practice massage in Russia, but I never will: I took classes simply to learn how to give better massages here, in the mixed bath.

Friends offer to give me massages here. I like to give them back.

Beneath my hands I can feel Oksana's heart beating slowly, powerfully. I am careful not to press near the base of her spine, which is crooked from when, as a girl, she was dropped by a boy as he tried to throw her into a lake.

Around us others, too, are giving and getting massages. Some women are standing, rubbing coffee grounds over their skin, making the skin soft, opening the pores to receive the honey that they will smear over their thighs, hips, stomachs, breasts, shoulders, arms, foreheads and cheeks. They will wear the honey into the steam room, where it will be absorbed entirely by the skin. When they walk out, their skin will no longer be tacky, but soft, aglow.

This is something for which the Church once imposed penance. In the eighteenth century it was accursed for a Russian Orthodox believer to rub honey into the skin; this also held true for salt, oil, milk, hops, human blood, and even dew. This evening, though, some of the women wearing honey also are wearing small gold crucifixes on chains around their necks.

Metal basins clang on cement slabs. Flip-flops slap through shallow puddles of water. Shouts, laughter echo off the walls of the washroom.

My hands are moving over Oksana, but my thoughts turn to myself. I am leaving the country in several weeks on a slow road from Eastern to Western Europe, then on to the United States, to southern New Jersey, to the one-square-mile town where I grew up.

It is a drawn out departure for someone fond of long hellos and short goodbyes.

Again I am moving somewhere without a return ticket, without a job, and without a clear aim. Only this time I am not nervous, or scared. I am not excited, either.

There will be plenty of Russians nearby, in Philadelphia, and plenty of Russian speakers. There will be banyas, too—on the outskirts of Philly, as well as in northern New Jersey and New York City. But this does not happen in those banyas. There, men and women wear bathing suits. And there is no Viktor.

He is already inside the steam room when Oksana and I return, languid, for the last collective steam. She tells me I should go up to the deck, where the steam is hotter, more intense; she thinks she is holding me back. But I have experienced enough intensity, enough sensations, for the evening. I want only to stay low, to stay warm, with her.

"Quiet, quiet," Viktor says. "Let's talk later, all together, okay?"

He says he is about to guide us through what he calls psychological training.

"Quiet, that's enough my friends. That's enough now, silence. We breathe in deeply the good, moist, Russian steam. We breathe out." We rap on each other between the shoulder blades to the sound of *om*. We progress through a sequence of sounds—*aaah, ohhh, oooh,* and *iiii*—before inhaling to *ikh*, a sound we make thirty-two times in swift succession "so that our soul excurses along our body."

Water is hurled into the stove. Instead of a clap, and a burst of steam, the water sizzles as it evaporates from the rocks. The stove, like us, is tiring.

"Now, quiet. We shut off the lights in our eyes, close them. Our body has remained here. Now let's travel a bit, let's dream a bit. We listen only to my voice, and envision what I am going to say. Each person has his own associations."

"Your boss," he says.

"Now imagine him in our banya."

Laughter.

"Yeah, there are many problems with people's superiors.

"Now your subordinates.

"And now picture them in our banya."

Water is cast into the stove.

"And now picture yourself." He pauses. "Picture what Clean Thursday means in Christian mythology. Now picture ablution in the Ganges River, in the Vedas," the ancient collection of Sanskrit poems, or hymns, that are sacred to Hindus.

"And now, just for a moment, picture Lake Baikal," the lake in southwestern Siberia, the oldest and deepest in the world, which holds one-fifth of the world's fresh water. "Shamans, shamanic Mana near Lake Baikal. We take a deep breath. Above us is the starry sky, beneath us is the abyss. And us? We are all together, at the center of the universe.

"We conjure up our favorite drink, take a sip, and another. We take a bite of our favorite food. Steam emanates from us, as if tiny bumble bees are inside us, and we know that we are the best. We hurl ourselves into Lake Baikal. Below us is the abyss, and above us is eternity."

"The steam is summoned!"

For the last time water crashes against the rocks. There is a faint concussion, the sound of water changing its molecular structure, changing what it is, entirely.

Steam, the last of it, erupts from the rocks.

"Thank you!"

Applause.

The Banya Is Communion
«Баня—это общение»

Another soldier of the Japanese imperial forces was discovered the other day, alive. He was not in a jungle on a remote island in the Pacific, rifle at his side: Ishinosuke Uwano knew the war was over, for he had been among the more than half a million Japanese soldiers taken prisoner by the Soviet Union. He was last sighted in 1958 on Sakhalin Island, in the Russian Far East. Over the ensuing years he married and raised a family in the former Soviet republic of Ukraine. He could not return to Japan "because of the former Soviet regime." Or so he says.

"I just don't want to talk about it," an eighty-three-year-old Uwano told reporters during a visit with relatives in Japan. "It was simply a matter of fate. Ukraine has become my homeland."

Uwano was captured involuntarily, but went missing by choice. The Japanese government—which officially declared him dead—believes another several hundred imperial soldiers are still alive in former Soviet space. Like Uwano, they found reasons to stay.

I was drawn in to his story because, until recently, I, too had found reasons to stay. His story also reminded me of a good, but seldom-seen friend, an American who effectively has gone missing not in Ukraine, but in Russia. John has no intention of going back. Russia is his home.

"I don't consider myself an expatriate. I'm a transplant," John once told me. "By the time I die, I'll be one of perhaps only a handful of people who have done this."

By this, he means moving to Moscow in the 1980s and living through glasnost, the period of openness, and perestroika, the period of reform, and then the collapse of the Soviet Union, and then the harsh, hardscrabble beginnings of the Russian Federation, and then the country's materialistic, authoritarian, and corrupt advent of the twenty-first century.

Most Westerners come here for work. They are paid good money, often exceptional money. They do not stick around for all that long, though, and rarely learn how to converse freely with their drivers, housekeepers, and nannies.

John is a theater critic and author who came here on a Fulbright Scholarship and stayed, at first, for a girl. He knows the language so well that he translates new Russian plays into English. He earns little money. He has found a number of reasons to stay, one of which we share: something of a dependence.

A dependence on what? On chaos.

Chaos is a state—disorder, bedlam, pandemonium. It also is a scientific theory. The theory holds that systems rely on an underlying order upon which even minor events can have major, seemingly disproportionate, impacts. An example is the one about the flapping of a butterfly's wings in South America creating a change in the atmosphere that influences a pressure system over the Caribbean Sea that forms into a hurricane that touches ground in the United States.

John would say that Russia feigns order while all the time relying on an underlying disorder. "You are constantly in a battle to keep going here. There is a sense in this country that I am in touch with living, that I'm actually engaged in the act of moving forward in space and time because I'm constantly getting racked up."

The underlying order of Russia is its chaos. The near absence of social protections. The ineffectiveness of rules and regulations. The unresponsiveness—nay, indifference—of government. The dangers, literally life-threatening, inherent to politics and business and the exercise of one's civil rights. Even in the sidewalks.

"By American standards, the sidewalks are atrocious. There are slabs of concrete sticking up four or five inches, and the steps are made unevenly," says John, a tall fifty-something with a beard and frizzy, graying brown hair. "I was asked once in the States, 'What do you do if you trip on the sidewalk?' And the assumption was who do you sue? And I said, 'What you do is, if you trip on the sidewalk, you just remember next time to watch where you're going. You get up and walk on.'

"For me, that little vignette says a lot about this country. This is a country where you have to watch where you're going. . . . If you have to watch where you're going all the time, you're paying closer attention to your life."

Friends who have gone back to the States say the same things, only not in those words. At first it is a relief, they say, life working the way it is supposed to work. It is pleasant, reassuring. It also is comparatively static, boring. When friends tell me they miss Russia they really are saying they miss the electricity of living more for the day, of finding themselves in situations where they must take more risks, and rely more on their intuitions.

"Maybe I'm sick, maybe I'm crazy, but there's something in the battle itself that makes me feel alive," John says. "It's too easy in the States."

It takes a toll, the chaos. Drinking and smoking and poverty and bad ecology are not the only reasons people here look markedly older than their ages. Still, life as it is lived here has rarely allowed me to disengage, to feel as if I am a spectator to my life—the way I felt before I left a staff job with career trajectory at a newspaper in southern California for unemployment and uncertainty in Moscow.

I had planned to stay only a year. But I became rooted to Russia by its chaos.

It is not a coincidence that I am leaving now, for chaos has been receding under the rule of Vladimir Putin. His rise to power came as Russians had had their fill of imperfect democracy (often they refer to it not as *demokratiya*, or democracy, but *dermokratiya*, or crapocracy), and many were nostalgic for the security and stability of a strong Soviet hand. Putin looked and acted the part, even if his regime was not nearly as strong as its Soviet predecessors. Most Russians were willing to pretend. They still are.

Today they are less free, less open, less fun. But their country is less chaotic.

An irony in all this is that, by always leaving myself open for the possibilities presented by chaos, I left myself closed to others. I walked away from the greatest love of my life because I did not want to marry and become a parent. I declined several entreaties to become a biological father. I did not buy real estate in Moscow when it was affordable. And I did not look far beyond journalism for work that would tap into the country's wellspring of so-obscene-it's-hard-to-fathom wealth.

While rooted to chaos, I did not put down other roots.

John did, though. Just about the only thing he retains from his old American life are framed newspaper clippings and black-and-white photographs of him stretching for line drives while a third baseman in the minor leagues after being drafted by the Oakland Athletics baseball team. They hang from a wall in his first-floor apartment in downtown Moscow—the kind of place that several years ago sold for $60,000 in cash, and today would net more than a quarter million dollars. Also in cash.

Everything else he needs is here. He is an authority on the theater of the country in which he lives. He is married to the highly-regarded (and pretty) actress, Oksana Mysina. He holds the Russian equivalent of a Green Card.

Without such traditional footholds, though—and without chaos—I have few reasons to stay. So I am leaving. And John is staying.

"I continue to have full confidence in the power of Russian chaos," he told me. "I believe I'm very safe that Russian chaos will win out."

Surely chaos was at play when, upon telling him that I had embarked upon the long goodbye that became this book, he smiled, and said: "I know what you need to do. You need to go visit a friend of mine in the Urals. You need to go to Banya Lake."

Banya Lake? I am tempted here to lay out another theory—that of inevitability.

Of course there had to be a Banya Lake in Russia. The lake is said to have gotten its name in the 1770s after Emelyan Pugachyov, the Cossack leader, staged a collective bath on its shores for his peasant army. Pugachyov posed as the late Tsar Peter III during his rebellion against serfdom and the rule of Catherine the Great—who was still married to Peter III when she helped to overthrow him, and became his widow when he died, mysteriously, while in custody. Pugachyov overran much of the territory between the Volga River and the Ural Mountains before he was betrayed by his fighters and delivered, in a cage, to Moscow—where his head was lopped off and his body quartered.

Banya Lake, or *Bannoye Ozero*, is what Russians call the lake. The native Bashkirs, who speak a Turkic tongue, call the lake *Yakty-Kul*, or Clear Lake. John vacationed there with Oksana while judging a theater festival in the nearby steel city of Magnitogorsk. Friends of one of his friends own big houses on the lake. Surely, John said, they must also own banyas.

He sent an e-mail to his friend, a theater director.

Sergei, the theater director, wrote back.

"Today I opened my mail, saw your letter. I'm actually going to the birthday of one of my friends today, and will ask the guys. You must understand that it will entail a specific quantity of drinking, and I'll ask if anyone is up for [a visitor]. . . . After all, the banya here, you understand, is not only an external influence on the body, but a corresponding influence on the internal organs. All the best, don't forget! Hugs, Sergei."

A few days later Sergei writes, again. He and the guys are up for a visitor. Not only that, they have come up with a plan: I will fly into Magnitogorsk, where we will hang out and steam casually at a private sauna-cum-banya, then we will all travel to Banya Lake, in the neighboring republic of Bashkortostan, where we will steam hard in one or more of the guys' private banyas.

I write back to Sergei, accept his invitation.

John was right. Again, Russian chaos wins out.

I have traveled among the Ural Mountains, but I have never been to Magnitogorsk. The city is known colloquially as Magnitka, and it is to Russia what Pittsburgh is to the United States. It is more like three Pittsburghs, really—or a half dozen, maybe more. It is hard to quantify the importance of a city that produced every second tank and every third shell for the Red Army during World War II. In fact, the city's colossal metallurgy plant supplied the Soviets with enough iron and steel to help push the Nazis all the way back to Berlin from the Western Front, the thousand-mile stretch along which nearly four million Wehrmacht troops, and some twenty-seven million Soviet soldiers and civilians, perished.

And if the Soviets had not repelled the Nazis, the Allies almost certainly would not have won World War II.

Today Magnitogorsk also is known as one of the most polluted places to live in the country (a distinction linked, too, to the metallurgy plant). It also is seen as a truly Eurasian city in that it straddles the Ural River—the left bank of which is Europe, and the right bank of which is Asia. Or so people say. The river serves as a sort of dividing line within the dividing line that are the Urals, a north-south mountain range along which Russians break the country into two. To the west is Eastern Europe, the Caucasus Mountains, and the Baltic Sea. To the east is Siberia, the Far East, and the Sea of Japan. Russians call the western part of the country "the European half." They rarely, if ever, call the eastern part "the Asian half"—a reflection of its sparse population (only fifteen million, or some 10 percent of the population, lives there) and chauvinism.

There is more to Magnitka than its metallurgy plant and its place on a map, but not much. The Magnitogorsk Iron & Steel Works (MMK) accounts for some 95 percent of the city's revenue, and employs most of its 415,000 residents. All of the city's trolley tracks lead to the plant. All of them.

It takes a little more than two hours to fly from Moscow to Magnitka. In the run-up to my flight I pack light, leave enough space in my carry-on for a half dozen tightly bound bags of exotic coffees from the best supplier in Moscow; coffee beans are widely available these days in Russia, yet, while the aromas are seductive, the quality of the roasts usually is poor. I also slip into my carry-on printouts of the latest news available online about the city.

I learn that a seventeen-year-old male stole the cell phone of a younger male on Mayakovsky Street. A Model 10 Zhiguli passenger car, or *desyatka*, was stolen, too, from a locked garage; police believe it is being hidden nearby in another garage. An unidentified man, thin, about forty years old, wearing black slacks, a gray coat, and a black hat, died when he was run over by a trolley after falling onto the rails on Saltykov-Shchedrin Street. The cost of a one-way ticket on public transport just increased to eight rubles, or some thirty-five cents.

I fall asleep on the Tupolev Tu-134 while awaiting takeoff, and awake after the plane has begun its descent. It is a rude awakening, for the turbulence is so severe that the plane falls sharply, fitfully, to a point not far above the Ural River. I recognize the river as the winding ribbon of black against a field of tungsten-toned street lights.

I look out the window to avoid the fear on the faces of other passengers. I am not yet nervous even though I am aware, of course, that Russia has the world's worst air safety record. I also am aware that the record pertains primarily to Western planes, for which there are too few highly qualified pilots and mechanics. We are flying in a second- or third- or fourth-hand Tu-134, a Soviet aircraft built from 1966 to 1984. Plenty of Russians can fly, and fix, a Tu-134. The heightened air pressure in the cabin blunts the elevated whine of the engines in my ears. In the thin space beneath my reflection I watch as a building on the riverbank catches fire. The flames seem to encounter some kind of accelerant and, within tens of seconds, engulf what appear to be three other buildings. It is a serious fire.

The plane touches down heavy and hard. As it taxis toward the airport terminal I send a text message to Sergei, who insisted on meeting me even though it is the middle of the night.

He texts back, "Hurrah!"

Sergei has not asked what I look like. Most Russians who meet me at airports, or trains, do not ask. They assume I will somehow stand out, will somehow look American—even though, over the past decade, I have unlearned my American ways so completely that police no longer stop me to check my documents.

I know that Sergei is tall, with dark hair. I notice him before he notices me. I walk over, smile a close-mouthed, un-American smile. He smiles, too—only big. I am suddenly self-conscious.

He drapes an arm over one of my shoulders, tilts his torso toward the other, and drops his head.

This is how Muslim men greet each other in the North Caucasus, the volatile region in the country's southwest. There, the greeting once was explained to me as a means of expressing affection that enables men, without offense, to verify that the other is not holding a weapon behind his back.

Sergei is not Muslim. He is merely from the theater.

He has a large nose, short black hair and smallish dark eyes that convey a sensitivity to, and a proclivity for, suffering—more often than not, I suspect, at his own hands. I take to him immediately.

He insists on carrying my bag. We walk to his car, a white Volga sedan that runs on both gasoline and natural gas. I suggest skirting the riverfront because of the fire.

He sparks a Marlboro Light.

"That can't be," he says in Russian, "I just came from there."

I tell him what I saw from the plane window.

"It can't be, it can't be."

It can, it can.

But Sergei is right: there is no fire when we shadow the river in search of a hotel (the room Sergei reserved for me at a new chi-chi place was rented out from under us). The flames were from an enormous pile of slag that was expelled, in stages, from the metallurgy plant. I am anxious to see the plant in daylight.

We settle on the Asia Hotel, where I am put in a suite with a kitchen and two bedrooms, one of which is occupied by a man whose dress shoes—shiny and black, and square at the tips—are sticking out from a wardrobe in the foyer. I cannot sleep soundly because, every half hour or so, prostitutes knock on the door.

At some point in my sleeplessness I hear the door shut, followed by a woman's voice, hushed, and the sound of a zipper from a tall boot. My suite-mate apparently could not sleep either.

I do not hear the long zipper again, as I am sleeping soundly when its owner dresses, and leaves—for the knocking has stopped.

I shower before my roommate with the shiny, square-tipped shoes. Then I dress, walk outside to wait for Sergei. He insisted on picking me up, showing me the city.

I sit on a curb next to a playground where hand-carved wooden sculptures of *bogatyri*—epic heroes akin to knights—rise up from coarse sand. From the hotel name I divine that I am loitering on the eastern bank of the river, in Asia.

In the space between two apartment buildings I see the metallurgy plant, on the other bank of the river. Only a small section of the plant is visible, yet I count twenty-six smokestacks. Three stray fingerlings of chalky pink smoke rise staggered against a backdrop of collective exhaust that has turned the sky the hue of moldy skin on an apricot. In the foreground white smoke roils from a cooling tower, a man-made cumulonimbus big enough, I suspect, to have obscured much of the mountain from which the city got its name.

Magnetic Mountain—not a mountain so much as two bare hills—was taken down over the past century, scoop by scoop, by miners.

Deposits of iron ore were discovered here in the 1740s, but the city only really came into its own in the 1930s, when Joseph Stalin—in a bid to achieve military and industrial self-sufficiency under the First Five-Year Plan—set about creating a "Soviet Pittsburgh." The early years were chronicled by John Scott, an American who, at age twenty, escaped the Great Depression by moving to the Soviet Union to work in the heralded "new society."

A subsection of the fifteenth chapter of his book, *Behind the Urals*, is comprised of one paragraph: "This was the Magnitorgorsk of 1933. A quarter of a million souls—Communists, better-off peasants, foreigners, Tatars, convicted saboteurs and a mass of blue-eyed Russian peasants—making the biggest steel combine in Europe in the middle of the barren Ural steppe. Money was spent like water, men froze, hungered, and suffered, but the construction work went on with a disregard for individuals and a mass heroism seldom paralleled in history."

The early Magnitka was a showcase for socialist urban planners, a place "without churches, without taverns, without prisons," to borrow from the lyrics of a local song. The city would be closed to outsiders because of its critical role in the military-industrial complex. Later, in the 1930s, much of the plant's administration was arrested during Stalin's purges (even John Scott was nudged out of the country), and, again, during World War II. From the curb on which I am sitting much of the war-era infrastructure appears still to be in use.

I am distracted by the reflection of bright gray daylight from the newly cleaned windows of a first-floor apartment across the street. I think of the person on the other side of the glass: How much will does it take to be so meticulous downwind of the plant?

Sergei arrives in his white Volga. I hop in. The car is aptly named after the river, for it rides like a boat.

Sergei and I do not talk. I roll down the passenger's side window to let out the smoke from his cigarette, then roll it up as quickly: like a log in a flume the car is being sprayed with water that is rushing, brown, along the streets.

Sergei looks over, says, "Spring!"

The onset of spring is brown in most of Russia. It does not mean flowers, tree buds, and grass. First the snow must melt and, as it melts, it reveals, like an archaeological dig, all that accumulated over the seven or eight or nine months of winter weather. Empty cans, plastic bottles, glass bottles. Packaging for dried fish, potato chips, ice cream. Cigarette butts, dog feces, and nutrient-bereft dirt. Temperatures today are in the thirties. Water from the banks of swift-melting snow, their peaks frozen in scale-model bridges of granular ice, collides in rooster tails at intersections, at the bottoms of hills. It carries off loose chunks of asphalt. It splays silt over the white of pedestrian crosswalks.

We drive past a fancy new hotel, then across Karl Marx Prospect, where two girls are traversing puddles in tight jeans and high heels. We pass a new Russian Orthodox cathedral, one of only two in the city, before climbing a small hill, at the top of which police are measuring the distance between two cars that crashed head on.

Another driver comes upon the scene and brakes, too late. The car rams into one of the damaged cars, which rolls into yet another car.

"Look," Sergei says, "broads behind the wheel."

The sun is already high in the sky when we pass the indoor hockey rink where, tonight, Metallurg will vie for a place in the finals of the Championship of the Russian Superleague. We pass tall rows of apartment buildings made of prefabricated concrete slabs, stacked. We pass a statue of Vladimir Lenin standing on a pedestal, hand extended.

He is wearing a proletarian cap and an overcoat. He is chubbier than usual.

Sergei pulls up to a cluster of low apartments with rustic stone facades and ornate wooden eaves. He turns off the engine.

The apartments are Soviet. Yet, unlike most things Soviet, they are well-constructed, and tasteful. Sergei tells me the complex is called the Little Italian Courtyard, or *Italyansky Dvorik*, because it was built in the 1940s by Italian and German prisoners of war.

We get out of the car, walk around. "When I'm really feeling down, totally miserable, I come here with a small bottle of vodka, or a book, and I read, watch the leaves fall," Sergei says. "It's so great here."

Sergei is not local. He was raised in the far northeastern region of Chukotka, where his father worked as a geologist. He moved here a few years ago in order to make his bones as a theater director upon graduation from the Russian Academy of Theater Arts (GITIS), in Moscow, where he studied under the famous director, Pyotr Fomenko. While the provinces yield the country's best contemporary playwrights, the best directors continue to be trained in Moscow and St. Petersburg.

"I'm seen as kind of a big shot," Sergei tells me.

His theater, the A. S. Pushkin Magnitogorsk Drama Theater, is named in honor of Aleksandr Sergeevich Pushkin—the poet and ladies man with mutton-chop sideburns who was shot dead in a duel, only to live on as the greatest Russian writer, ever.

Pushkin lives on more as a god, really.

Back in the car we crisscross the city, pull up next to a construction site where two of Sergei's friends, Andrei and Rafael, are building a high-rise business center.

Sergei kills the engine, lights a cigarette.

"They are real millionaires," he says, referring not only to Andrei and Rafael, but his other friends with banyas on Banya Lake. "I knew them for six months before I learned they had money. They are those kinds of people, just good guys."

Millionaires did not really exist, certainly not openly, until the early 1990s. It still means something to know a millionaire in Russia, even if society has become less impressed: more and more the benchmark is billionaires, of which some thirty-six reportedly possess a quarter of the country's wealth.

Sergei says he has never sought donations from the guys even though the theater is owned by the state, and financing is skeletal. "They are not sponsors or anything like that, but that does not stop them from volunteering their help from time to time. If they hear that something is not right, they can step in. But we are friends, just friends, and I want to keep it that way."

The windows are down and the air feels incongruously fresh, light. I watch the afternoon sun reflect in muted colors off the faded paint of buildings. I feel happy to be away from Moscow, happy to be hanging out with Sergei while tooling around a city that not long ago was closed to foreigners, even those from Communist states, as well as most Russians.

Sergei has given me a sense of place, as well as a real sense of connection. He has set the stage, as it were—which, perhaps, comes naturally to a theater director.

Later that day I meet Sergei at the theater. I give him and his staff some of the exotic coffees; the gift, which seemed appropriate when I bought it, now strikes me as meager.

He and I take a cab to the main offices of Andrei and Rafael, where we wend our way along a first floor corridor until we reach a door that opens into a large room where Andrei, wearing slippers and a white sheet tucked around his waist, greets us.

Andrei is slim, light-haired. He smiles more with his eyes than his mouth, which releases words in rat-a-tat bursts.

"One day," Andrei says, "we were sitting around in another banya and we asked ourselves, 'Why not build a banya for ourselves? We would see each other more often that way.'"

So he and Rafael renovated a wing of the building to accommodate not only a banya with an electric stove, but a Turkish-style steam bath, a plunge pool, a massage room, and a Russian billiards table. They chose billiards over pool, Andrei says, "because pool is over too quickly, which means I'm not able to drink as much."

At first they steamed too often, every other day, Andrei says. "Our wives were like, 'Maybe you say you're steaming, but you're really ordering in girls?'"

The billiards table is the centerpiece of the room, which has shiny black ceilings and walls of wood and stone. It also has a modern kitchen, a faux fireplace, and a large dining room table heavy with food. Smoked hunchback salmon. Roasted chicken. Kielbasa. Shrimp. Ham. Smoked cheese. Mayonnaise-based salads. Apples.

On two plates are small triangular pies, *samsa*, stuffed with pork, or chicken, or cabbage. There are pickles, too, and lemon slices intended to complement the drinks—mineral water, fruit juices, two kinds of Czech beer, and a vodka I have never tried, Green Mark, which is distilled with Siberian pine nuts.

"Vodka without beer is like money in the wind," goes a popular Russian expression. (*Vodka bez piva, dengi na veter.*)

There are five of us. Two other guys in sheets, Dmitry and Oleg, are seated at the table. I am taking notes, which makes Oleg uncomfortable. I tell him it is the only way I can be sure to get things right.

I even recite a Chinese proverb, the one about the palest ink being better than the most retentive memory.

Really, I say, I am taking notes for a book. I give you my word.

"There is nothing more dangerous than people who give their words," Andrei says.

Someone fills five shot glasses with the vodka. We toast to acquaintanceship, to *znakomstvo*, and drink them down. We reach for something to eat. I snatch a pickle.

It is not so much that pickles go with vodka, which they do, but it is customary in Russia to eat something, anything, after downing a shot. Bread. Fruit. Dried fish. Marinated mushrooms.

Eating while drinking means one is less likely to get drunk. It also means one is able to drink more.

A television station is already broadcasting the game between ours, Metallurg, and theirs, Avangard. Our team has cheerleaders, girls in sexy pink outfits. Our team also has a mascot, someone in a furry fox costume. The score is tied, 1–1.

Metallurg has had a strong run of success. The team recently won the Euroleague and repeated as champs of the Russian league. Lately, though, they have been underachieving.

"To the puck! To the puck!"

I tell the guys that I cannot drink much tonight—should not drink at all, really—because I am taking antiviral medication. My words are to little effect, for soon we are downing another vodka shot, lending credence to the popular expression, "Between the first and the second is a small interval."

It rhymes, in Russian. (*Mezhdu pervoi i vtoroi promezhutok nebol'shoi.*)

There is a small interval between the second and third shots, too, but this is not in keeping with any sort of custom: we are simply drinking fast.

The third toast is to health. Andrei says that the third toast—traditionally the most meaningful in Russian drinking hierarchy—is always to health. Yet that is not the case everywhere I have been in Russia. Often I have drunk to love, or to family. An ex-girlfriend's father, a former submarine commander with whom I regularly drank vodka, always proposed the third toast "to those at sea."

Sergei promised a mild steam, and it is. Between successive shots we drift into the banya, then cool off in the pool, then drift into the so-called Turkish-style steam bath, where the steam is so heavy we cannot see others' faces, then drift back to the table—to drink, to talk, to watch the game—before meandering back to the banya.

The guys call the main steam room a banya, but, really, it is a sauna with an electric stove similar to those found in spas and fitness clubs.

So far tonight's steam resembles more the initial encounters between Russian businessmen and their foreign counterparts, during which the banya experience—accompanied, as a rule, by heavy drinking—is simultaneously a test and a means of establishing some degree of trust.

In the steam room with Sergei and Andrei I ladle water over the rocks and, as if on cue, I begin to sweat torrents. My body has ceased to bother with nuance in regulating how it sweats over the past several years. I suspect it is a consequence of steaming often, and deeply, in the banya. I only wish it better understood the difference between a steam room and the stale warmth of the Moscow subway.

The temperatures in the steam room tonight are not high enough, really, to warrant wearing a hat, but I could not resist plucking from a rack a white felt hat in the style of a Viking helmet—with faux horns and, between them, a patch depicting the Playboy bunny.

I ask Andrei about his earliest memories of the banya. One's experience at the banya as a child often determines the degree of passion he holds for the banya as an adult.

Andrei says his earliest memories date back to the seventies. He was seven years old and his father took him to a public bathhouse once a week, to wash.

The bathhouse was adjacent to a wooden barracks where eighteen families lived in eighteen rooms. Men went on Fridays, and women went on Saturdays. Andrei always stayed low in the steam room, where it was cooler, while the men steamed on benches close to the ceiling, where it was hot.

Andrei says he came to like the banya because "there are no generals"— that, naked, everyone is equal. He regards the Russian banya as a combination of the best of the Finnish sauna and the best of the Turkish bath, or hammam.

The hockey game goes into overtime. Metallurg has talent, flourish, but Avangard has intelligence, patience. More importantly, Avangard has luck. The visitors win, 2–1, on a freak goal after the puck ricochets off the boards, off one of the goalposts, and off one of the goaltender's pads, into the net.

"Vermin! Germans! Fascists!"

Fists are pounded into cushions. Someone mutters that hockey is an insufferable game.

Dmitry lights another bowl of tobacco, says, "You start out with a pipe, and you end up with who-knows-what."

We begin to play Russian billiards, which is a lot like pool only the pockets are narrower and the balls are white, save for one, the cue ball, which is red. Any ball, though, can serve as the cue ball over the course of a game.

The door to the room opens, and guys who were at the game walk in. Someone belts out (it might have been me), "*Shtrafnoi!*" The word means penalty, and it is what one says to those who arrive late to a party. It usually entails drinking one hundred grams, or a small juice glass, of whatever everyone else is drinking.

We are still drinking vodka.

Andrei's business partner, Rafael, is among the newcomers, but he refuses to drink because he is taking medicine for a growth on his foot. Rafael's older brother, Ruslan, says, "I haven't had a drink for two weeks. I sure want to drink. If I wake up and I'm not sick, then I haven't had enough to drink."

Someone proposes a toast, the sixth. Or maybe it is the seventh. We drink to change, to our personal development—with the caveat that we always will remain friends.

Sergei says people do not change, only their views.

Someone says an Armenian thought up the ballpoint pen. Someone else says the inventor of alcohol had a Muslim surname. Another says, "The more you drink, the farther you go." It is a well-known Russian expression, the meaning of which is beyond my grasp.

Rafael lifts a guitar onto his lap, tunes it matter-of-factly, and begins to play a popular song from the eighties. The guys sing along but I do not, as I cannot remember the words. I begin to feel as if I am observing the table from afar.

I feel, too, a sort of lightening, an awakening in my chest. I do not know whether to attribute it to the alcohol, the steam, or the sense of communion I am feeling with men who, only hours ago, were strangers.

Rafael plays and sings another song, then another. He passes the guitar to Dmitry, who used to perform, solo, in cafes. Like the others, he is self-taught. He has the best voice.

I am recording the moment on my digital camera and, as I pan across the table, Oleg turns his face.

A red light on the camera begins to blink: the memory is low. I stop recording and start deleting images from my latest visit to the States, images of my mom and three younger sisters—images I have yet to save elsewhere. By the time I resume recording Dmitry has passed the guitar to Ruslan, who admonishes everyone to "stop acting like fools," and to listen.

His voice is guttural, yet melodic—a lot like the song he is performing. It is called "Summer Downpour," but it is not one of the popular compositions that carry the same name. It is so good that we cannot help but shut up, and listen.

Goose bumps run down my arms, and across my shoulders. I am suddenly aware that I have not stopped smiling for a long time.

In Moscow I do not smile this much in a week.

Or even a month. Probably longer.

It is nearing four o'clock in the morning and most of the food has been eaten, most of the bottles have been emptied. None of us has to work later today, except for Ruslan. On the way out he downs yet another shot of vodka, one for the road. If he wakes up and is not sick it is because he is not alive.

Andrei's common-law wife picks up Andrei, Sergei, and me in a late-model Peugeot. We drop Sergei at home. On the way to the hotel Andrei tells Larisa to turn off a main street onto a dark, empty road. We follow the road around traffic circles, and across railroad tracks, past a lone, poorly lit kiosk with bars over glass behind which are displayed cans of alcoholic cocktails, bottles of beer, cigarettes, salty snacks, chocolate bars, and chewing gum.

Farther along Andrei tells Larisa to slow, to put down the windows. The interior of the car is overcome by a sulfurous scent. Andrei urges her on, around a bend, where we see a kind of mountain—not the one from which the city got its name, but the accumulated discharge of decades of production at the metallurgy plant.

Under stadium-style lights bulldozers are navigating its undulating ridge, pushing heaps of the steaming mass over the edge, growing the mountain.

The slag glows a dark orange. Steam rises as if from a peat bog in early morning.

This is what I saw on fire, from the plane.

"Imagine, seventy years ago this was nothing but steppe," Andrei says. "It's a very bright city now. Fifteen years ago it was dark. They wouldn't even let in Poles or Bulgarians, let alone spies, or agents, like you."

He is not smiling.

"It's a very capitalist city despite all the statues of Lenin. How much it's changed over the past fifteen years! I don't know if you even want to bother going around, gathering up your secrets."

Some spy. I cannot even remember the lyrics to popular songs. I have a hard time with names, too; Sergei glared at me earlier when I mistakenly called Andrei, Aleksei.

I do not say anything.

We backtrack along the twenty-square-kilometer perimeter of the plant, toward downtown. Andrei tells Larisa to pull over at a large public square, in the center of which burns a gas flame. Beyond the flame, facing west, is an enormous bronze monument depicting two men steadying a sword, horizontally, over their heads.

Andrei says it is one of a series of three memorials to the Soviet victory in World War II. The first is here, he says, because it symbolizes where the sword was made; the second is in Volgograd, where the decisive battle that carries the city's former name, Stalingrad, claimed the lives of nearly two million German and Soviet soldiers, as well as civilians; and the third is in Berlin, where the sword was thrust into fascist soil.

Andrei stood guard over the flame as a member of the Komsomol, the Soviet youth organization. Back then kids nicknamed the monument, "Hold this while I take a piss."

Andrei gets out, opens up the trunk, grabs a beer.

He offers one to me. I shake my head.

"It's true," he says, "I like to drink."

If so, he is able to drink and function at an extremely high level. I have not earned in a decade as much as he told me he collected last year just in stock dividends.

That year the metallurgy plant raked in some $1.2 billion in profits. While the average Magnitogorchanin earns about $1,000 per month, there are enough people in the city with enough money to warrant a direct flight between Magnitogorsk and . . . Zurich.

The director of the plant, Viktor F. Rashnikov, is reportedly the ninetieth richest person in the world.

By the time Andrei and Larisa drop me off at the hotel the trolleys have begun their runs. I apologize to the key woman—some Russian hotels have preserved the Soviet-era practice of designating clerks to hold room keys, usually on each floor—for waking her. She says she does not mind.

"I thought I lost you," she says.

The roommate I never saw is gone. No one is knocking, for soon the sun will rise, and even the prostitutes are asleep.

In the afternoon I again meet Sergei at the theater to wait for a ride to Banya Lake. It takes about forty minutes to get from here to there, in Bashkortostan.

The republic was called Bashkiriya under Soviet rule, and many ethnic Russians continue to call it that—out of habit, and a low regard for the will of the Bashkir ethnic minority. The republic is best known in Russia for its honey, which is said to be rivaled only by that from the Altai region of Siberia. I have eaten honey from Bashkortostan that was derived from the nectar not only of flowers, but trees and roots, such as ginseng.

Until recently politicians in Bashkortostan—who administer government less along the lines of the constitution than those of their respective clans—managed the economy the old-fashioned way: use whatever natural resources are here, while they are here. These days there is talk of reinvestment, of a sustainable economy.

A dark blue Mercedes pulls into the theater parking lot. Behind the wheel is Nikolai, one of the friends who arrived late last night because he was at the hockey game. On the way out of the city we stop at a wholesale market. I ask to go in, to help shop.

"No, no, wait here in the car," Nikolai says. "I'll put on a good Russian song for you." He slips into the CD player a recording by the folk group, *White Day*, whose female vocalist uncharacteristically yields to the accordionist.

I move to hand Nikolai some money. For the beer, I say.

His expression turns sour. "Do you want to offend me? Please, don't."

Thus far I have paid only for the hotel.

We are traveling on a well-paved road beyond the outskirts of the city when Nikolai says that he is still coming to grips with something Andrei said last night. "I run every day, not less than eight kilometers. This morning I ran ten kilometers. And yesterday, [Andrei] goes, 'You can run every day, every day, and your belly still is the biggest of all of ours.' I wasn't ready for that, morally."

Nikolai does not have a big belly, certainly not by American standards. If anything, he is slight of build. From the back seat I remind him that, yesterday, my belly was biggest.

I strikes me that last night's remark cut to the quick because it indirectly assaulted Nikolai's will. For many years he smoked, and smoked heavily. Eventually he quit, in part, through jogging. To this day he wakes up early and plods for miles and miles over dirty streets, in dirty air, and, for much of the year, in the serious cold of dark morning.

Will appears to be the common denominator in the lives of all of Sergei's friends, the ones with banyas on Banya Lake. Last night Andrei even remarked that he has exceptional willpower.

It is not by accident that they have prospered at the same time many Russian men have come undone while trying to make the transition from the Soviet Union to the Russian Federation. Everywhere there are men who have been left behind by the times like heavy machinery abandoned by a swift-moving army. Some of these men were acquaintances of mine. They coped, literally, by drinking themselves to death.

Nikolai runs a company that is somehow linked to the plant. It is probably one of the thirty independent subdivisions that were created in 1992 when the plant registered as a joint-stock company. But I am not sure, and I do not ask. After last night, I have resolved not to be inquisitive in ways that might cause others to presume I am someone other than who I am.

Nikolai is fair-haired, almost naïve in his enthusiasm and good humor. He is forty-nine, and his wife is twenty-three. They have a four-year-old son. Not long ago they opened a café downtown called The Big Changeover, or *Bol'shaya Peremena*.

I tell him that the name is a good metaphor for his life, as well as that of the city.

In the rearview mirror I see him smile.

He begins to recount for Sergei and me a rafting trip he took last summer with friends. One day, he says, after making camp on a riverbank, they built a so-called field banya, or *pokhodnaya banya*, the most primitive of all banyas.

They gathered dry rocks and arranged them in a thigh-high pile in the style of a bread oven on the riverbank. In the hole they built a fire and stoked it, stoked it, stoked it before waiting for it to burn down to coals. They scooped out the ashes. Then they erected a squarish tent around and over the pile of rocks. They brought in fresh-cut boughs of birch, and pine, and laid them on the ground around the rocks. Then they got naked, and got inside.

Someone began to ladle water over the rocks. The water sizzled. The rocks made popping sounds. The steam wrested from the leaves and needles their essence, swept it up into the moist air. When Nikolai and his friends became too hot they waded into the river, or unzipped a flap in the roof of the tent. They did this, heated and cooled, heated and cooled, till each person's body told him he had had enough.

"You have to understand," Nikolai says, "dinosaurs once walked over those rocks. When you pour water on them, it's . . . a connection, a conversation with nature. The rocks give you what they hoarded up over the centuries. And what can release that energy, that energy stored up over millions of years? Fire. Heat."

"When you finish [steaming] you realize, you feel—yes, I'm still a man!"

Nikolai (right) and friends have traveled extensively by raft along the waterways of the Ural Mountains. They make camp on riverbanks upon which they also build field banyas, or *pokhodnye bani*, in which they wash and steam. Stones are piled over a fire they stoke for hours, and hours. When the stones are hot enough, coals are removed and a square tent is placed over the stones. Bathers cool off by wading into the nearby waters. Credit: Nikolai

We pass a metal kiosk on the side of the road. It is the size of a railroad car, painted yellow. In red paint it says Tsarist Fish.

We approach a mountain upon which ski trails are chiseled, white, like the scarce veins over a heart. We follow the devolution of the mountain into tree-lined hills, then bare hills, before arriving at a lake that sits in a crater-like depression.

Banya Lake is about three miles by one and a half miles, but it looks smaller. Its surface is covered by a rough layer of ice over which are sprawled shallow puddles of water, yellowish in tint. The water is alkaline, salty. For centuries it has been used to help heal skin conditions.

We follow the narrow road that hugs the shoreline past kiosks, grocery stores, small hotels, even the village's former communal banya, which wound up in private hands and was converted into a sauna—a V. I. P. sauna, or so a sign claims. It is a long way from the ancient banyas of the Bashkirs, who threw animal skins over tree limbs lashed together above a pile of rocks—much like the field banya described by Nikolai. The former communal bathhouse is the kind of place one no longer goes so much to steam, but to spend time, by the hour, in a so-called room of relaxation—a small room with a big bed and, likely, a big mirror on a wall.

We pass dilapidated wooden houses that stand at the far ends of rectangular plots dedicated to growing cabbage and potatoes, and bounded by waist-high picket fences. Around a bend, beyond a fence shrouded by brush, sits Nikolai's house on the water.

It costs more to build on the shores of Banya Lake than it costs to build on coastal Spain, or so the guys tell me. Nikolai bought his house twelve years ago. He shakes his head, "To this day I still can't believe I have this house."

Certainly it was not part of the adult dream of a boy in the Soviet Union to own a one-story bungalow with wood siding and a tile

This lake in the republic of Bashkortostan is known as Banya Lake, or *Bannoye Ozero*, in Russian, and Clear Lake, or *Yakty-Kul*, to ethnic Bashkirs. In winter puddles of mineral-heavy water, yellowish in tint, spread across the ice.

dipping pool from which one emerges, through sliding glass doors, onto a secluded patio where a stone barbeque stands tall like an idol to a faraway god. In the Soviet Union men waited well into their thirties, even forties, for a poorly made car.

Nikolai's banya is being renovated. We will steam later in the banya situated high up a hill, the banya with smooth timbers the color of caramel that overlooks the terraced backyard of a gray stucco house with an ornate window that delivers light into an atrium three stories high. The house and the banya are Andrei's.

"That's already Turkey up there," Nikolai says.

He is referring not to an architectural style, but to a notion: Turkey holds a place in the collective consciousness as one of the countries to which Russians could travel easily in the nineties for their first taste of a vacation beyond the Communist pale.

Indeed, Andrei's house and banya look foreign among the modest homes and even more modest banyas of those who have yet to be bought out, or pushed, from the shores of Banya Lake. The juxtaposition reflects generations worth of change in less than a generation—for bathhouses like Nikolai's and Andrei's did not exist, not really, when I first moved to Russia.

Only over the past decade has it become fashionable to build banyas so exclusively oriented toward leisure, and not living. I call them trophy banyas. Paradoxically, they are appearing at the same time the country is reclaiming its roots—re-staking banyas in private, rural plots and, in doing so, pulling the energy of the cult of steam away from the large public bathhouses of the cities.

While public bathhouses have been falling sharply in number, the country has been experiencing no less than a banya boom among those with the means to build on land they can now own. These banyas are not one's parents' banyas: they are often designed to distinguish oneself from one's neighbors. "Everyone wants a house in the country, and, if you own your own house, as a rule it has a banya," Lyudmila Nikonova, an ethnographer in the republic of Mordovia, told me. "It's no longer acceptable to simply use your neighbor's banya."

Nikonova attributes the resurgence, too, to healthier lifestyles and a growing interest in herbal remedies.

Andrei's wooden banya sits high on the shores of Banya Lake, in a fenced-in property Nikolai says is reminiscent of the notion of travel to a foreign land. A stone plunge pool sits behind the circular patio, or sitting room. In winter, spring water and beers are chilled in snowbanks.

Historically, couples lived in banyas (one can sleep on the benches, and use the stoves for cooking and heat) while the main houses were built. Today banyas are among the last things homeowners build. These contemporary banyas—well-built, well-lit, unblemished, and hygienic—are the private banyas I know best. They reflect wealth, yet they are not the richest in their contributions to Russian bath culture. Certainly I cannot picture them as ad hoc operating theaters for "the ones who know," or *znakharki*, typically women of middle age or older who practice Russian folk medicine, which is primarily herbal.

"Ones who know" have persevered through centuries, through times even when bathing with herbs was an accursed practice for which penance was imposed. A *znakharka* (or *znakhar*) might possess a stock of seventy-seven or ninety-nine herbs, roots and berries

The banya of Rafael, with its vinyl siding, is less remarkable than that of his friends, but his year-round pool—with its panes of clear and blue glass—is like none other.

that were gathered when they were believed to be most powerful—at certain times of the day, like morning, when leaves are coated with dew, and at certain times of the year, like Midsummer or on the women's feast day of Agrafena the Bather, *Agrafena Kupal'nitsa*, when dreams are said to be more prophetic, and divination with herbs more potent.

"Every ailment has its herb," goes the Russian proverb.

These days most every Russian knows he can down a glass of vodka with garlic or pepper, take a bite out of an onion, then go off to the banya, to steam, as soon as he begins to feel sick. Still, today, most other forms of folk medicine are administered over a counter by a pharmacist—except, perhaps, in provinces where people live much as they did before the 1917 revolutions that ushered in communism. There, healthcare continues to revolve around steam rooms. In fact, these remarks by António Nunes Ribeiro Sanches, a Portuguese physician in the court of Catherine the Great, are as relevant today as they were in 1774: "I, for my part, regard only the Russian banya, prepared in the proper way, capable of delivering to a person such great benefit. When I think of the variety of drugs dispensed by pharmacies and chemical laboratories, . . . half or three-fourths of them . . . could be replaced by the Russian banya."

Remedies might call for an herbalist (*travnitsa* or *zeleinitsa*), or a sort of chiropractor (*kostoprav*), or even a midwife. More often than not, though, folk remedies involve "one who knows."

Sometimes a *znakharka* incorporates benign spells and magical prayers into her rituals, which is why, in some regions, she is called a *sheptun'ya*—a title derived from the verb, to whisper (*sheptat'*), as spells are typically cast by whispering over agents such as water, alcohol, butter, bread, salt, or tea. Such spells, like bathing with herbs, were outlawed as recently as the late eighteenth century.

Ritual purification and physical cleanliness seem to go together, which is probably why folk medicine in Russia long has been intertwined with magic. In fact, Russians historically would have seen little difference between magic and medicine. "There are many charms and prayers . . . in which the addition or omission of a word or two makes all the difference between a licit prayer and a magic spell," writes William F. Ryan in *The Bathhouse at Midnight*, his breathtaking survey of divination, magic, and witchcraft throughout Russian history.

"It takes a shrewd theologian, however, to distinguish miracles from magic, and most ordinary people of any period would have seen no difference."

A *znakharka* nominally does not go so far as to invoke spirits, or perform malefic magic. Darker, blacker magic is left up to wizards and witches, who to this day practice magic primarily to gain wealth, power, and sex. Magic also is used to exact revenge, and to protect oneself from someone else's magic.

Like banyas, like folk medicine, magic has experienced an uptick in Russia since the Soviet collapse. Still, irrespective of the ebb and flow of magical practices over the centuries, the communal village bathhouse and midnight have persisted as "the conditions par excellence for popular magic and divination in Russia," Ryan writes.

Even a contemporary Russian book on magic insists that the banya is the best place to become a witch, or wizard. I cannot envision magic being practiced in trophy banyas, though, for there is nothing dark about them.

Certainly I cannot see wizards sneaking off to a trophy banya while everyone else is at church. I cannot see one being used to harbor a wizard, either, like Prince Vasily Golitsyn purportedly did in the late 1600s while trying to conjure magical love spells to attract the Regent Sofia. And I certainly cannot picture trophy banyas as places where young girls might gather to divine the names and physical appearances of their future husbands, something historically done during the winter (from Christmas Eve to Twelfth Night) and green (Trinity week) holy days, as well as the summer solstice and various feast days.

A close reader of Russian literature might already be aware that teenage girls used bathhouse rituals to try to determine the material worth of a potential husband, or even the direction from which he would travel. Sometimes they poured boiling wax into water and held the resulting shapes up to a flame, reading the shadows on a wall. More often than not, though, they set a table, for two, in a bathhouse. The ideal time for this, naturally, was midnight.

In Lev Tolstoy's novel, *War and Peace*, an older woman recounts one girl's experience to Natasha and other girls over dinner:

> "No, fortune-telling in the bathhouse is scary!" the old maid living with the Melyukovs said over dinner.
>
> "How come?" asked the oldest daughter of the Melyukovs.
>
> "You wouldn't go to such lengths. It takes courage . . ."
>
> "I'll go," said Sonya.
>
> "Tell us what happened with the young lady," said the second Melyukov girl.
>
> "Well, it happened like this," said the older woman. "The young lady went alone—with a rooster and two place settings, as is customary—and sat down. She was sitting for a while when, suddenly, she hears something approach . . . a sled with jingle-bells and sleigh-bells. Then she hears him coming. He enters in the perfect likeness of a man, as a military officer, just walked in and sat down before the place setting."

"Ah! Ah!" shrieked Natasha, rolling her eyes in terror.

"Yeah, right—a man. He could actually talk?"

"Yes, like a man. Everything was as it should be. And he got up, he got up and began to woo her. She needed to keep him engaged in conversation until the rooster crowed; but she lost her nerve; she simply lost her nerve and covered her face with her hands. And that's when he grabbed her. It was a good thing that the maids ran in at that very moment..."

A table for two in a bathhouse also figures in Pushkin's verse novel, *Eugene Onegin*, in one canto of which Tatyana and her nurse conspire to conjure an image of Tatyana's future husband—only for the girl to get cold feet. Instead, she goes to bed and has a strange dream:

> Tatyana, on the advice of her nurse,
> Planned to divine all night.
> She quietly ordered a table set
> For two in the bathhouse;
> But Tatyana suddenly became scared ...
> And I, with thoughts of Svetlana,
> Became frightened, too. Very well, then ...
> Tatyana and I won't divine our fortunes.
> Tatyana untied her silk sash, undressed
> and got into bed. Above her hovers Lel [god of love—b.m.],
> And beneath her down pillow
> Lies a girl's looking glass.
> All is quiet. Tatyana sleeps.

A looking glass, or hand mirror, beneath a pillow was another way girls hoped to see the future. Yet this ritual, like a table set for two, has fallen away over time. Some bathhouse rituals have kept on, though, among them two of the most intriguing: prenuptial ritual baths, and childbirth.

As recently as 1971, in the northwest region of Vologda, Ryan writes that a wizard (referred to as a guard, or *storozh*) led the bride to her ritual bath with a fishnet around his waist, then massaged her with bundles of leafy birch twigs while reciting the spell, "On this birch besom the leaves will never go away. The same will happen to God's servant Yekaterina, the husband will never go away from her. Amen."

The bride's sweat was then wiped from her body with a raw fish, which was cooked and given to the groom to eat.

Sometimes a charmed thread was wound around a bride's body during her ritual bath. Other times—as, again, in the Vologda region—the bride wore clothes into the steam room that were later burned, the ash of which was sprinkled on the husband's food while the following spell was recited: "As this shirt was on the body, so may the husband be to the wife."

Men had prenuptial baths, too, but they were pretty unremarkable, as little remarkable has been written about them. This is surprising in that banyas figure more prominently in the lives of Russian men, according to Igor Kon, the country's foremost sexologist.

Yet even if the banya plays a bigger role in the lives of men, banya culture has been most richly decorated by the contributions of women. They are usually the "ones who know," not to mention the herbalists, the midwives, the bone manipulators. They often gather the *veniki*, often stoke the stoves. As girls, they venture into banyas to perform rituals at times when even grown men would stay away. And for centuries they have even given birth in steam rooms— lending a literal dimension to the well-known saying, "The banya is your second mother."

Historians say the practice of giving birth in steam rooms likely arose as a consequence of poverty, and a corresponding lack of living space. But that does not explain why women at the court of the seventeenth-century tsars also gave birth in banyas. (Princess Olga in 946 even used the steam room to avenge the death of her husband, Prince Igor. When a delegation of Drevlians—the Slavic tribe that killed him—arrived to ask for her hand on behalf of their prince, she had a bath prepared, as was customary, and locked the banya once the emissaries were inside. Then she ordered it set ablaze.)

Part of the reason women gave birth in steam rooms surely had

This 1889 painting by Aleksei Korzukhin depicts a so-called *devichnik*, or bridal shower (also bachelorette party), which typically takes place the day before the wedding. The bride is shown clutching a white sheet, in the doorway of the bathhouse. Credit: Wikimedia Commons

to do with the banya as a source of warmth, and hot water. Moreover, blood and other fluids could simply be sluiced past the gaps between floorboards, or down a drain. And whereas heat kills microbes, in early so-called black banyas—in which there are no chimneys—the soot that covers the ceilings and upper walls serves as a natural disinfectant, providing a safer environment for babies and their mothers.

As in prenuptial baths, men do not really figure in childbirth rituals. However, a rare account from the early nineteenth century, in the northwest region of Smolensk, speaks of a man lying on a bench above his pregnant wife, a thread tied around his penis. "The midwife would jerk the thread to coincide with the woman's birth pangs," Ryan writes, "thus producing sympathetic cries from above."

Princess or peasant, a woman in labor was never left alone in a bathhouse. The *bannik* is said to dislike women in labor. The same holds true for the one-eyed old lady of the banya, the *bannaya babushka* (also *baennitsa*), another of the domestic demons.

For this reason, among others, a midwife would stay with the mother during labor. Sometimes she would disrobe and carry a newborn around the exterior of a banya while chanting an invocation to the dawn, or the Morning Star, to keep the baby from crying. *Znakharki*, too, cast spells to make babies fall asleep, or stop crying. (Babies who were weak, or suffering from rickets or hernia, would be "rebaked" by placing them on a bread peel and sliding them three times into a warm stove, or oven.)

Today childbirth in banyas is rare, but not unheard of. Several years ago a longtime friend of mine gave birth to a daughter in a steam room. The banya in which she gave birth was not a trophy banya, though. I cannot imagine such a thing happening in such a banya. It is almost as if today's banyas have different souls.

Still, even if trophy banyas are less suited for living, they are better suited for socializing—for the communion that buoys the relationships among Sergei and his friends, and for which I have flown some 870 miles.

Sometimes communion, more than anything, is why I steam. It is enough on its own. It can be more than enough.

I packed my hat, flip-flops, and wooden folding seat for the banyas on Banya Lake, but I have yet to unpack them: anything anyone might need for steaming is already here, in Andrei's banya. Felt hats. Felt gloves. Flip-flops. White linen sheets. Bundles of leafy birch and oak twigs. A rustic wooden table holds a liter and a half of Johnny Walker Black Label Scotch Whisky, a liter and a half of Putinka vodka (the brand appeared out of nowhere shortly after Putin appeared, also out of nowhere, on the national political scene), some gin, some tonic, and some naturally carbonated mineral water from the Kamchatka Peninsula, a disneyland of natural wonders in the Far East.

I know everyone seated at the table, except one. He is a ranking boss at the plant, a former athlete who carries the title, master of sport, in track and field. He is still fit, and handsome, with thick brown hair worthy of genetic decoding. Even though he is roughly the same age as everyone else, all refer to him by his first name and patronymic, Igor Ivanovich.

I am jotting down the brand names of the liquor when he leans over, tells me in a serious tone of voice, "Alcohol and the banya are incompatible, by the way."

I am reminded of the popular Russian expression, "He who doesn't smoke, or drink, dies healthy." (*Kto ne kurit, i ne pyot, tot zdovorenkii umryot.*)

Igor Ivanovich is right, of course. Yet booze and the banya have more in common than five letters. One of the most beloved Russian movies, the Soviet comedy *The Irony of Fate (Or With Light Steam)*, begins with men drinking vodka, on New Year's Eve, in a public bathhouse. (The movie is shown nationwide on television on New Year's Day, much the way *It's A Wonderful Life* is shown on Christmas, in the States.)

Andrei gets up from the table to stoke the stove. He opens the hatch and a howl fills the room. He stabs in more birch. The wood catches fire instantly, the flames bending muscularly against the uppermost bricks. The stove was recently designed and built by scientists from Akademgorodok, or Academic Town, the enclave on the outskirts of the Siberian city of Novosibirsk. The town was founded in the 1950s as a sort of incubator for the best minds of the Siberian branch of the Soviet Academy of Sciences. But, these days, most all of the dozens of scientific institutes are underfunded, and most all of the researchers have died of old age, or retired, or left the country.

Of the stove Igor Ivanovich says, "The scientists didn't have anything better to do. But, like everything in Russia, it wasn't exactly what was needed: it is too strong, too powerful, just too much."

When the steam room is hot enough Sergei offers to massage me with bundles of birch, and I agree. From a bucket in the washroom he grabs a *venik* in each gloved hand, shakes out excess water from the rehydrated leaves. He walks into the steam room, and I follow.

I take off my sheet and lay it flat on the lower of two benches made from a light ash. I lie on my stomach, tilt back my Kyrgyz felt hat—finely brushed white wool embroidered with a national pattern, in black, with a small black tassel. I rest my forehead on my hands, close my eyes.

I hear Sergei ladle hot water onto the rocks, which sizzle. Lightly he begins to strike the soles of my feet with the leafy *veniki*. His touch is feathery; I feel only the softness of the outer leaves, not their collective heft. Slowly he works his way up my legs, pausing intermittently to raise the *veniki* toward the ceiling—moving them in clockwise-counter-clockwise waves that push the hottest air over my skin while infusing the leaves with more heat.

I wince. The stove truly is potent.

Sergei ladles more water onto the rocks. Again he lifts the *veniki* toward the ceiling, twirls them, brings them down simultaneously onto my upper back and shoulders.

One-two, one-two.

The *veniki* emit a sort of whoosh-thwap-slap as they collapse against my skin. Sergei works his way down my spine in a quickening rhythm.

One, two-three-four. One, two-three-four.

The blows are fleeting, but their effects resonate even after Sergei has moved on to other parts of my body.

His breathing begins to sound labored.

Again he raises the *veniki* to the ceiling. He shifts them to one hand, then brings them down onto my lower back. He holds them there, pressing down with both hands—pushing the warmth deeply into my body. Sergei lifts one of the bundles, reaches it toward the ceiling, twirls it, then places it behind my knees. He grabs my ankles and bends my calves upward, toward my back. He holds them there for about fifteen seconds, long enough for the heat from the leaves to pass through the thin skin and travel along my calves, to my ankles.

I underestimated Sergei. I thought he was here more for the party, and less for the steam. But his movements in the steam room are deft, intuitive. Toward the end of the massage he says his offer was not entirely selfless: "When you need to warm up quickly, it is better to beat someone else than to be beaten."

Sergei leaves, and I follow him out—my skin pink and wet, my mouth slightly agape. I, too, feel somewhat winded. At the same time I feel a spike in energy: something powerful is at work inside me.

In the washroom I stand beneath a large wooden bucket hinged to the ceiling. I pull on a chain and the bucket tilts, dousing me with frigid water. The bucket refills automatically.

I douse myself again, and again. The water feels warm by the time it reaches my ankles.

I am slicking the water off my body with my hands when I hear Nikolai's voice from the other room. He is saying that we should be discussing not only the dynamics of the banya, but interpersonal relationships.

As I return to the table he says, "You know why I love Rafael? Because he finds something good in me. The same thing with Sergei."

Sergei does not appear to be listening. He is reciting an expression that claims it is better for a man to drink vodka than beer because, from beer, the blood becomes bitter, and the cock droops. (*Ot piva krov' kisnit, i barsik vysnet.*) It rhymes, in Russian.

By now we are comfortable enough with each other that Sergei has become Seryozh, or Seryoga. Andrei is Andrush, or Andrushechka. Rafael is Rafik. Nikolai is Kolya, or just plain Kol'.

Igor Ivanovich is . . . still Igor Ivanovich.

And I remain merely Bryon.

Some Russian friends call me Bry, or Bryonchik, or Brayosh, or Brasha, or Brynusik, or Brynusechka. (A male acquaintance, gay, calls me Bryonikha.) But my friends and I have known each other for years, whereas Sergei and his friends have known me for little more than a day.

I get up from the table, walk outside to the snow bank that encircles the plunge pool. I retrieve a bottle of a dark Czech beer, Golden Pheasant, from the hard snow. When I get back someone is suggesting replacing all the Lenin statues in Magnitogorsk with statues of local heroes. The consensus is that the idea is good, but ahead of its time: we must wait until all the Soviet-era Communists die.

Someone else offers up a joke about the Russian character:

Three soldiers—a Russian, a Frenchman, and an Englishman—are captured by the enemy. They are offered a choice as to how they want to die: by hanging, by firing squad, or by guillotine.

The Frenchman, naturally, chooses the guillotine. Only, when the rope is cut, the blade fails to drop. The enemy chalks it up to fate and sets him free.

On his way out the Frenchman whispers to the Englishman that the contraption is broken and, naturally, the Englishman chooses the guillotine. Again the blade does not fall and, again, the prisoner is freed by his captors.

On his way out the Englishman whispers to the Russian that the guillotine is broken and, naturally, the Russian chooses the firing squad—because the guillotine is broken.

Between steams we talk more, and drink less, than last night. The talk and steam have already wound down when the door to the banya opens and Larisa walks in with a friend, Lyudmila, a petite blonde who owns an upscale shoe store.

They are all smiles. And so are we.

As we say our goodbyes the guys and I agree to steam once more late tomorrow morning at the banya of Igor Ivanovich.

The girls, Andrei, Sergei, and I move from the banya into Andrei's house, where we talk and drink and play ping-pong, and Russian billiards, until around five o'clock in the morning. Outside the door of my room are a pair of sneakers. They are Rafik's, a reminder that I incautiously promised to join Igor Ivanovich and Kolya for a jog . . .

. . . in less than three hours.

I wake up on time, but I cannot keep pace; the last time I ran for health was seven years, and twenty pounds, ago. I muddle through four kilometers in the time it takes the guys to run eight. I should feel wretched from drinking too much, and sleeping too little, but I do not. I attribute it to the mountain air, and to the banya.

Back at the house I give Andrei the last of the coffees. I feel somewhat self-conscious, as I have not paid for anything since Magnitogorsk; Andrei even intercepted me yesterday at a cash register and insisted on paying for my snack.

I am accustomed to paying my own way. Growing up my family had little money, and I have held regular paid work since I was eleven. I later lived on my own, and worked two jobs, while still enrolled in high school. But I do not stand on principle here, in the Urals: I accept the generosity of the guys as sincere, because it is.

If Andrei treats a spy this well, then he is a man without enemies.

We walk to Igor Ivanovich's house, which is constructed almost entirely of large timbers. The design is echoed in his banya, which sits in the yard among saplings of white birch and pine.

Banya Lake squats below. Mountains crest at the horizon.

Igor Ivanovich already has begun to heat the stove, which he says reaches an ideal temperature after two hours if the logs are birch; other woods take longer. The stove is about the size of a keg of beer, on its side. Its metal walls are five millimeters thick. Two hundred and sixty-four pounds of volcanic rock are piled on top.

This is Igor Ivanovich's second banya. The steam room in his first banya was heated by an electric stove, which he says burned up the oxygen, dried out his mouth, and killed off even healthy microbes.

He likens a first banya to the first pancake in a batch: always imperfect, and always tossed out. "Everyone dreams of building his own banya," he tells me, "but if you build one banya, you'll build another for sure."

There is no alcohol on the table in Igor Ivanovich's banya, only

The wooden banya of Igor Ivanovich overlooks the tops of white birch growing up the sloped shores of Banya Lake, which is bounded by mountains opposite. The property has yet to be landscaped.

a big white teapot in which black tea leaves are already steeping. The guys are subdued; only athletes, perhaps, steam as often, and as hard, as we have over the past few days.

I feel comfortable, confident in this banya—which bucks popular lore in that Igor Ivanovich is clearly in charge, and none of us is his equal.

Among Sergei's friends Igor Ivanovich is the most ardent in his passion for the banya. He has been steaming some thirty-six years, since he was ten years old. After steaming he never showers with soap, or shampoo, but simply rinses off with water so as not to clog his open pores with chemicals and perfumes. He prefers to steam in the evenings because he does not feel rushed. Accordingly, he says, there should never be a clock in the banya.

"I hung up a clock once," Andrei says, "and it promptly broke."

Briefly my thoughts turn to the *bannik*, the goblin of the bathhouse.

Igor Ivanovich says he steams once a week, either on Saturday or Sunday. Usually he steams with his wife, Lyudmila.

"My sons also love it," he says.

He offers to beat me with two bundles of oak, and I accept.

"There are different ways to steam," Igor Ivanovich says, "but only an idiot sits there, without *veniki*, and does nothing."

In the steam room Igor Ivanovich wields the *veniki* with agility, varying the tempo of the blows. He begins at my feet because we jogged this morning. At times he presses both bundles together to deliver heat directly to specific parts of my body. He calls this method a "thermo press."

"We recently had a family tragedy," he says. "My son was killed in a terrorist act."

The older of his two boys, Aleksandr, was shot eight times, three times in the heart, while traveling in Venezuela.

"The wife is taking it very hard."

Igor Ivanovich stops massaging me and climbs to the bench closest to the ceiling, sits down. He beats his upper arms and chest with one of the *veniki*. Then he holds the *venik* in front of his face and breathes deeply through its leaves.

He says his sons helped him design the banya.

"The boys love to steam, too."

His thoughts seem to carry him to another place.

I am about to recite a Russian expression akin to, "Allow me to express my condolences," but stop myself: here, in the steam room, the words seem so impersonal as to be insincere.

I do not say anything.

Igor Ivanovich slides to the floor and stands in the middle of the steam room as if he is being searched at an airport. He begins to whack his torso, his thighs, with both *veniki*. He exhales softly with each blow. He leans forward slightly and beats his lower back with one of the bundles, the part of his banya ritual he says he likes most.

I offer to massage his back with the *veniki*. He shakes his head.

We leave the steam room. I am hot, but not so hot as to want to jump into the icy water in a large wooden cask. I fill a plastic basin with cool water, instead, and pour it slowly over my head and shoulders. I do this three times.

In the room with the white teapot I wedge myself into a corner of one of the sofas, my sheet open at my chest, which rises and falls as my body cools, as my heartbeat returns to normal. I am not paying close attention to the conversation, but perk up when I hear someone say, "Non-alcoholic beer is the first step to a blow-up doll."

For the next couple hours we talk, and steam, and joke. Most of us drink mineral water and hot black tea sweetened with sugar. Some of us drink lager-style beer. At one point Nikolai offers to give me photographs of the field banya he and friends built during the rafting trip.

From my corner of the sofa I realize that the banya has been one of the main reasons I have stayed in Russia as long as I have. Of course there was the sexual revolution—theirs, and mine. And there was interesting work. And travel. And friends. But more than anything, perhaps, there was the banya.

John, the American theater critic, has his reasons. Uwano has his. And I have mine.

Igor Ivanovich pours himself a mug of tea. He looks youthful in his fluffy white terry-cloth robe. I think I can envision how he looked as a boy. He walks outside, and I follow him out.

We rest our arms on the railing of the veranda. Between loud, bubbly slurps of tea, Igor Ivanovich talks of the banya. I listen.

Sometimes the steam is so good, he tells me—the physical euphoria so great, the communion with others so soulful—that it feels like "one of those days, those times, when you look back and can legitimately say, 'Wow! That was one of the best days of my life.'"

The Banya Is Holy
«Баня—это святое»

It is late afternoon on the shores of a bay named Prosperity, but it might as well be late morning or, even, late evening—for these are the White Nights, the time of year when the sun never sets on this remote archipelago of small islands on the cusp of the Arctic Circle.

I am standing on a patch of trampled grass in the open territory of a monastery as legendary as its legacy is indelible on the sacred and secular history of Russia. The monk before me is wearing an inelegant robe of heavy sackcloth, the black dye of which has yielded to the color of cassis. He is talking on one of three cell phones he carries in his pockets.

"Don't judge, don't judge," says a man swaying between us, spectacularly drunk and unwashed.

"Yeah, yeah, you have time for everybody, except us," a second man, also drunk and dirty, tells the monk.

The men want money, but only work is plentiful at the Solovetsky Monastery—especially in late June, during the scant period of warm weather on the islands.

Pings from ball-peen hammers echo among walls some twenty feet thick, and up ramparts some thirty-six feet high. Atop the cathedrals scaffolding encases wood-shingled onion domes, the white light off which reflects as a mildly tarnished silver.

The monk stops talking on the phone, presses down the antenna with a palm. He looks past the men, at me.

I introduce myself, ask if the monastery has a banya and, if so, could I see it?

The monk continues to look at me, silent. He is gaunt, in his early thirties. Sparse ginger and gray hairs appear at his jowls, disappear along his jaw line, then reappear at his chin, from which they creep cautiously to a length of about four and a half inches. The hairs fall like lines on a topographical map.

He tells me his name is Father Gerasim. Then he tells me to follow him into one of the dormitories that line the inside of the monastery's walls. We sit on a low divan.

"How are you going to convey what you learn?" he asks.

I tell him I try to let stories tell themselves. I am a reluctant narrator.

"You are not going to pass on evil?"

I am unsure how to answer that question.

I say I always try to be fair.

"Fair?" He pauses. "Have you ever tried being merciful?"

It is my turn to look at him, silent.

"The reason I'm asking," he says, "is that I also love the banya."

He smiles. "Let's go."

I follow him through a door, and then another, into a catacomb of red brick that creeps in at the shoulders the deeper we walk. We reach a steep stairwell, the steps of which we take in twos and threes to a landing. Father Gerasim withdraws to his cell, retrieves a wooden tray upon which sits a Chinese tea service of black clay. A square dish holds frustrated spirals of dried green leaves; smaller dishes hold dried cherries, and cubes of dried coconut. He sets the tray on a table between us, sits down.

"It's written that you never catch a fly while drinking tea," he says, smiling.

I ask him what the expression means.

"That's just what they say."

I had not anticipated such a warm reception. I showed up with empty hands, one of the first things expatriates in Russia learn never to do. I feel a bit uneasy drinking exotic tea and eating exotic fruit—luxuries in the Far North—from a man I presume has taken a vow of poverty.

Father Gerasim asks me to address him as *ty*, the informal version of the pronoun, *you*. He also asks me not to record his voice, or to take notes.

I ask him to reconsider.

"Let's not record me, and leave it at that," he says. "You can't pass it on, anyway. That's why there are paints. That's why there is music. Words can't convey everything."

I relive some of the wariness I feel about trying to capture with words aspects of banya culture that seem to elude them.

Father Gerasim removes the lid from the teapot, drops green spirals into the blackness. He replaces the lid, leans back in his wooden straight-backed chair. The gray of his eyes is diffused with a blue that looks as if it were applied by brush—a dab of watercolor paint to wet paper.

He says he misspoke when he told me about his passion for the banya. "For others it is a passion, the physical sensations. For us, in Orthodoxy, it is not what is outside, but what is inside . . . We are not warmed by the heat of the oven, or by flame, but by the spirit of Christ . . . We are already clean inside by the flame of Christ."

For him steaming is about stripping himself of dirt, of all evil, then leaving it to commingle with the water on the floor before it is ushered out by gravity, along rusting pipes, into the Bay of Prosperity.

"What's left? Cleanliness, all that is good."

After steaming, he says, he literally feels born again.

Historically, some monks in Russian Orthodoxy never, ever washed—only dabbed at themselves with a moistened cloth.

Still, the Church has played a considerable role in banya culture—from its condemnation of pagan rituals, and denigration of pagan gods, to its cultivation of baths at its monasteries to serve as ad hoc health clinics for the poor.

In fact, the first reference to a banya in Russian is found in the account by Nestor of the travels in the first century of Apostle St. Andrew in Veliky Novgorod, where he was said to have observed men and women steaming, together. In 996 Grand Prince Vladimir proclaimed banyas "a place for the marginalized," or *nemogushchy*—the poor, sick, aged, and disabled. And in 1090 Efrem, the last metropolitan of Pereyaslavl, built perhaps the country's first stone baths—introducing what some historians say was a Byzantine or, even, Roman element to indigenous bath culture. (The Russian Academy of Sciences has traced the origins of the banya to northwestern territories, near the Baltic Sea, from the Western Dvina (Daugava) River to Lake Ilmen.)

By then some monks reportedly were already versed in the teachings of Hippocrates. Moreover, clergy and laymen—both male, and female—"washed and steamed together," according to Russian historian Nikolai Kostomarov.

Father Gerasim tells me he steams once a week, on early Saturday afternoons, with the dozen or so monks in the monastery—one of the holiest sites in Russian Orthodox Christianity, and a place of pilgrimage.

One monk makes the steam for the others. The older, more venerated monks typically steam first. Before entering the steam room, Father Gerasim crosses himself once.

He was once like me, Father Gerasim says—*mirsky*, or of the lay world. In 1996 he moved to Great Solovetsky Island—at some ninety-five square miles, the biggest of the seventy islands in the archipelago—from the city of Lviv, in western Ukraine. He joined the brotherhood in 2001 for reasons he will not discuss.

"So, how about you?" he says. "Have you ever thought about adopting Russian Orthodoxy?"

I harbor a negative view of the Russian Orthodox Church. My opinion is colored by personal experience, primarily with Church officials in Moscow, where I volunteered at an unaffiliated soup kitchen on Church property, and cofounded a bimonthly Russian-language newspaper that homeless and needy sold on the streets. Our soup kitchen eventually was made homeless, too—by the Church, which favored a considerably wealthier tenant, the Railways Ministry. The experience reinforced my observation that, while good at restoring buildings left to decay by the Soviet regime, the Church is not especially good with people, foremost among them its followers.

To project my biases onto Father Gerasim, though, would be akin to holding an average citizen accountable for the actions of his government. Besides, I also empathize with the Church: few suffered more under the Soviet Union than Orthodox believers.

To this day the Church must endure the deep insult of infiltration by agents of the Federal Security Service, or FSB, the main successor to the KGB. Even its first post-Soviet patriarch, Alexey II, was a former KGB informant from Estonia who went by the nickname *drozdov*, or thrush.

This view of the Solovetsky Monastery from the Bay of Prosperity shows a newly constructed chapel in the foreground, and Transfiguration Cathedral—with its five wood-shingled onion domes—rising from behind the walls. Monks maintain a special *bratskaya* banya that is closed to lay persons.

I tell Father Gerasim that I was baptized Presbyterian, but am no longer religious.

He is asking, he says, because it is no accident that I have lived so long in Russia, which he characterizes as the last world power to harbor a robust religious spirit.

"We're all moving toward one God, just by different routes," he says. "Perhaps the banya isn't the real reason you've come to the Solovetsky Islands?"

The simple answer to his question is that I came here as an afterthought.

Only this morning I awoke in the mainland port city of Arkhangelsk, in the country's northwest. I had traveled there by train for more than twenty-three hours on a sort of pilgrimage: with more public bathhouses per capita than anywhere else, Arkhangelsk is the closest thing Russia has to a banya mecca.

The secular sanctification I sought, however, could not to be found, because it is not possible. The public banyas are in deep disrepair because of corruption, mismanagement, and the strains on state-run enterprises in a coarsely free market.

Only six of the city's twenty-four banyas are deemed safe for use. The others would meet minimum standards after repairs estimated at twenty million rubles ($740,000)—costs compounded by reported annual losses of eleven million rubles (a seven-fold increase over the previous year), back wages, several dozen creditors, an overdue water bill and ongoing investigations into dubious employee bonuses and services (an audit, a property valuation) that were paid for, but apparently never performed.

At the bathhouses that still work the city pays about sixty-five rubles per bather, per visit. Bathers, after various discounts, pay about thirty rubles per visit.

In short, every time someone steams in Arkhangelsk, the city loses money.

The only person I could find who would rise to the defense of the city's banyas is Nadezhda Nikolaeva, the former director, who promptly left town upon my arrival—literally hid from me—despite a previously scheduled interview. Nikolaeva, who recently retired after seven years, refutes the city's allegations of malfeasance in an article in the local newspaper—which she paid 15,000 rubles, or $500, to have published.

I know because 3,000 rubles went to its author, Aleksandr Chashchin, who told me.

"Don't think badly about me, I didn't do anything to deserve that," Nikolaeva is quoted as saying in *Pravda Severa*.

Her legacy may best be assessed by the condition of the city's best banya, Vologodskaya. There the water and walls of the plunge pool are green with scum, and the steam room is only the size of a large walk-in closet—without ventilation, and with a sawhorse-style electric stove powered by a crudely spliced cord that trails into a hole in a cement wall.

No one throws water onto the stove because no one wants to be electrocuted.

There, and at the city's other public bathhouses, electrical power regularly cuts out because of disruptions to the grid. "People calmly continue to wash themselves and steam in the light of kerosene lamps and candles," reports *Pravda Severa*, which covers local bath culture like American newspapers cover local sports.

It turns out that Arkhangelsk is not a banya mecca, but a banya babylon.

In fact, the only place where banyas are in good condition is on the outskirts of the city, at *Malye Korely*, an open-air museum of traditional wooden architecture. Among the windmills and churches and sidewalks—all made of the region's abundant "green gold"— are chimneyless black banyas staggered along a hillside. Most are built of birch (honed by ax, not saw, in keeping with local custom, because saw-cut wood rots quicker), and bleached gray by snow and rain and sun.

I had steamed only once in the country's steamiest place, but I was ready to leave Arkhangelsk. Still, I was not ready for another twenty-three-hour train ride. So I kicked around the city—drinking unfamiliar beers and eating unfamiliar fish, mostly salted—while awaiting an inkling of what to do next. I was considering taking up a local girl on her invitation to steam at her family's banya in the countryside when I saw a travel brochure for the Solovetsky Islands.

I knew little of the Solovki, as they commonly are known. I knew that the monastery—a red imprint of which is on the back of the 500-ruble note—once served as the prototype for Soviet labor camps; Aleksandr Solzhenitsyn calls the Solovki camp the "mother of the Gulag" in his book, *The Gulag Archipelago*.

I knew, too, of the large stone from the islands that sits on a marble pedestal in a park in Moscow across the street from Lubyanka, the headquarters of the Russian security services. The Solovetsky Stone is a memorial to victims of Soviet repression—and, at times, a repository for the empty beer bottles of Muscovites.

That was about all I knew, though. So when a spot opened up on the Soviet-era puddle jumper that made the forty-five-minute flight this morning to Great Solovetsky, I bought it.

It would be cool, I thought, to steam so far north on a remote archipelago with a cool-sounding name. It would be even cooler to travel here as a tourist, and not a reporter.

This black banya at the open-air museum of traditional wooden architecture, *Malye Korely*, is larger than most. Still, like all black banyas, it does not have a chimney. Smoke spills out of the doors and window while heating, leaving behind a black sheen of soot on the boards.

I have yet to fully answer Father Gerasim's question—what is the real reason I came to the Solovki?—when he offers to show me the monastery's *bratskaya* banya, the name of which is derived from the word *brat*, or brother.

Only not today, he says. I need to call him to set up a time.

On one of his three cell phones. In an ancient monastery. On a remote island sixty miles south of the Arctic Circle.

Father Gerasim leads me down stairs, through catacombs, to a door. He holds it open. As I pass over the threshold he suggests that I read the novel, *Notes from the Dead House*, by Fyodor Dostoevsky.

Only through Dostoevsky, he says, will I get close to understanding the Russian soul.

"Oh," he adds, "you also need to steam here, in the north, where there is . . . a real banya culture. In the south, there is no such culture."

Banyas in the north are more essential for life. They lift spirits, and preserve health, in conditions that not only make life difficult, but cut it short. Northern banyas are smaller; steam rooms take more time, more wood, to heat. Most of the country's richest banya rituals, and folklore, have been recorded by ethnographers in the north.

As it happens I have already reserved time for tomorrow morning at the island's most popular banya, which is located just around the corner from the house in which I have rented a bed for 350 rubles ($13) a night.

Father Gerasim reaches into his robes, hands me two chocolates in dark green wrappers that are imprinted with a red squirrel clutching a hazelnut. He shuts the door.

I stand still on the matted grass of the courtyard, quietly euphoric. The Solovetsky Monastery has a banya, and Father Gerasim is going to show it to me—going to give *mirsky* me a glimpse of an otherwise closed world.

The drunk men are gone. I drop to one knee, pull a yellow legal pad from my rucksack, write down as much as I can remember from the conversation. I unwrap one of my squirrels, eat her (*belochka* is feminine in Russian) as I start down one of the footpaths that crisscross the open territory.

Pale grasses with pale blue wildflowers whoosh against my thighs. I lift my chin high enough to block out the walls, the ramparts, from my peripheral vision. I cannot tell if the bright white above is one big cloud, or an absence of clouds, or a kind of heavenly ether.

I breathe in deeply. Instantly my lungs ache; I take only shallow breaths in heavily polluted Moscow.

I have seen the White Nights before—in St. Petersburg, and in the north of Sweden. I have never seen them this bright, though, for this long. Earlier a local told me that he can see a twinge of something—a lurch toward sunset, perhaps—between two and three in the morning.

In the 1920s Maxim Gorky, the Soviet writer, described the White Nights on the Solovki this way:

The clock reads midnight, but you don't trust the clock; it's light all around, the earth's daylight hasn't receded, and there isn't a star in the pale-lit sky. The white nights are more transparent here than in Leningrad [now St. Petersburg—b.m.], the sky is higher, farther from the sea and islands. . . . This strange sky has neither stars nor moon, and it looks as if there isn't really a sky, but that the earth has been dislocated and hangs in a boundless, empty place.

I pass Transfiguration Cathedral. The wooden shingles of the onion domes now have a gunmetal shine.

I walk along one of the walls—together they surpass a half mile in length—toward the Heavenly Gates, a sixteen-foot-wide passage that serves as both entrance, and exit. The walls form a pentagon with round towers on each corner, and two more towers on two sides. Each of the seven towers stands out from the walls, and each has a name—such as White, Dormition, Spinning Mill, Archangel. Each also has a cone-shaped roof topped by a cupola.

The walls are built of boulders. Smaller stones and bricks fill in the gaps. The boulders—some of which measure twenty-three feet long—were levered out in summer, but put in place in winter, after two to three hundred men dragged them over frozen ground. The walls narrow at the tops, their ramparts built of bricks from the monastery's former brickworks.

All this grew out of a hermitage founded in 1429 by an elderly monk, Savatii, and a younger (illiterate) monk, German, who traveled to the island over two days by *karbas*, a six-meter-long rowboat, to find the isolation conducive to lives of near-endless work and prayer. The monastery stands on the site of a former wooden fortress that regularly burned. In the late 1500s it was rebuilt of boulders, in part, to defend the motherland from roaming bands of Finns, Swedes, and Germans.

Years later, in 1854, during the Crimean War, it would even repel the attack of two British warships. But the monastery's biggest fight occurred in the mid-1600s—against the Church, itself. The patriarch laid siege to the monastery after the monks cloistered here refused to adopt changes, or reforms, to Russian Orthodox liturgy and rituals. The monks, by then labeled Old Believers, repelled the siege for eight years—eight—until they were betrayed by one of their own. Nearly all, some several hundred, were tortured and executed.

The monastery fell only one other time. The Bolsheviks killed Tsar Nicholas II and his family in the summer of 1918, and in 1920 the Soviets reorganized the monastery into a collective farm. The monks were expelled. This time they did not put up a fight. The new Soviet government—which had denounced religion as an opiate of the masses—floundered as management, however, and for the first time in several hundred years, the monastery went quiet. In 1923 the Soviets reopened the site as the Camp of Special Significance, or SLON—the mother of the Gulag.

The only overt sign of the Gulag I see is, literally, a sign—a large plaque on a wall near the Holy Gates that says that a dormitory floor has been given over to a Gulag museum, the first such museum I have ever encountered in Russia.

I pass through the Holy Gates, stop on the other side on a road of sandy dirt that hugs the shoreline of the bay. It is the only road on the island, as best I can tell: it loops and hooks, yet intersects only with itself.

One way the road leads up a hill to the tourist bureau in the former Arkhangelsk Hotel, where female prisoners arriving at the camp once were held while overseers—in true life or death moments—decided who to take as lovers, and who to assign hard labor. The other way the road leads to a modest village center, and the two-story wooden house in which I am staying.

I turn toward home, walk past the shell of a former hydroelectric power station, past a man-made lake that supplies the monastery with drinking water (and fish), past a long wooden barracks, and another barracks, and another. Seasonal laborers crowd the front doors—squatting on their haunches, flat-footed, smoking unfiltered Belomor cigarettes pinched between pointer fingers and thumbs. The barracks are old. They date back several decades, at least. They date back to the labor camp, I think.

From the road the island reminds me of a diorama—that of a ghost town revived by those who moved in after the prisoners, in 1939, were moved out.

I am reminded, too, of something I long have thought, but feel alone in thinking: Russia is engaged in an experiment to move into the future without reconciling its past.

I use the word "experiment" because I am not sure it is even possible, a nation reestablishing itself with its eyes closed to what came before. It is as if Russians are willfully imperiling their future with a time bomb of grand dysfunction that will fate the country to relive its misfortunes.

Russians do not share my concern. I sometimes think my awareness stems from my Americanness: I grew up at a time when millions of Americans were examining their lives with the help of therapists, and holding their parents and childhoods accountable for their adulthoods—inadvertently rewiring themselves to arrive in the moment after scuffing through the cinders of their pasts.

While Americans were casting light into shadows, though, Russians were opting to continue to move among theirs. Somehow they do not take personally the decades of repression that affected them, or someone close to them—a parent or grandparent, an aunt or uncle, a cousin or family friend. Between twenty and twenty-five million people were direct victims of Soviet political repression. There is no figure for those indirectly affected.

"The past is a bad dream to be forgotten, or a whispered rumor to be ignored. Like a great, unopened Pandora's box, it lies in wait for the next generation," Anne Applebaum writes in her book, *Gulag: A History*.

On the Solovki, however, the past cannot be escaped. Relics are everywhere, in plain sight.

No one, ever, has been held accountable for crimes that, if not for Hitler, would have been the worst of the twentieth century. There have been no official truth commissions here. And if popular will ever rises to a level where such a thing is even possible, the perpetrators would have to be exhumed in order to be seated in a witness stand.

"The monument will be built when we—the older generation—are all dead," said Aleksandr Yakovlev, former chairman of the commission that officially rehabilitated more than four million of the politically repressed, often posthumously.

Maybe.

To me, consequences of the nationwide experiment are already apparent. How else to explain 77 percent popular support for a president groomed by the KGB, the organization that—with its predecessors, the Cheka and NKVD—is most responsible for the second-worst crimes of the last century?

Russians say they learned all they needed to know when the curtain of secrecy began to be pulled aside in the eighties and early nineties.

"What is to be done? It's our history," a Russian friend in his mid-thirties once told me. "Enough already. It's time to move on."

And, really, who am I to say he is wrong?

I love living in a place where people dwell less in the past, and live more in the moment.

Around a bend in the sandy dirt road I see a Soviet-era passenger bus parked among tall grasses. The door is open. Inside, boxes of books are stacked on seats. Near the driver's seat are books on the Solovki, some of which are memoirs written by former prisoners.

One of the books is by Dmitry Likhachev—one of my favorite humans, ever. A noted academic, he lived through the two revolutions of 1917, the 900-day Nazi blockade of Leningrad, imprisonment in the Gulag, and two world wars. He died in 1999. More than anyone, he was regarded as the conscience of post-Soviet Russia.

While flipping through the book, *Reminiscences*, I learn he was imprisoned here, on the Solovki—not once, but twice.

There also are books by Solzhenitsyn and another former prisoner, Varlam Shalamov, whose well-known work, *Kolyma Tales*, I long have wanted to read.

Solzhenitsyn proposed collaborating with Shalamov on a history of the Gulag—an acronym for Main Camp Administration, or *Glavnoye Upravleniye Lagerei*, written *GULag* (ГУЛаг) in Russian—in which some eighteen million people were imprisoned in 476 complexes from 1929 to 1953, the year Joseph Stalin died. (Another six million were exiled during that period.)

Shalamov declined the invitation, though, because of ill health brought on by the seventeen years he survived in Kolyma, in the Far East, where more than three million people died in more than a hundred camps spread across an area six times the size of France.

Also in the makeshift bookstore is a copy of *Notes from the Dead House*, the book recommended by Father Gerasim—one of the few works by Dostoevsky I have yet to read.

I buy seven books, altogether. Several are by former Solovki inmates.

When I reach the house the front door is unlocked. Upstairs I hear snoring behind the door to my bedroom. I open the door, see a man—tall, thin, in his early forties—asleep on the other bed. One of his hands rests on a book titled, *Tell Me, Good Lord, My Path.*

I put down several of the books on my bed, then walk downstairs and out. At the produce shop down the road I buy a fresh loaf of brown bread, two half-sour pickles and a small square of dry sheep's cheese. I ask a woman behind the counter to slice the pickles and cheese and, surprisingly, she does. I ask, too, for some of the herring that is indigenous to the islands. The store is out of stock, though, ostensibly forever: the woman says Solovetsky herring has been overfished to extinction. I also buy a liter of red bog-berry liqueur.

Outside I lean against the narrow overhang between a shop and its foundation, something called a *zavalinka* in Russian—the place upon which villagers can sit for hours and hours, shucking sunflower seeds, or getting drunk, or simply watching passersby. I tear off a hunk of the heavy bread, scoop out the doughy middle, drop in slices of cheese and pickle, and squeeze it all together. I eat quickly.

Glued to a cement telephone pole several feet away is a handwritten flier in black ink on white paper: "We invite you to visit the Russian Banya. A big lounge. Swimming in a lake. A steam room of up to 100 degrees."

One hundred degrees Celsius is 212 degrees Fahrenheit, the boiling point of water.

A hand-drawn map depicts the banya as a black rectangle on the shores of a lake that, as it happens, also is called Banya Lake—and is apparently fed by a Banya Creek. At 800 rubles ($30) for two hours, the banya, which is not named, is relatively expensive.

I am alone, and frugal—a word for which I have yet to find an oft-used equivalent in Russian that is not a synonym for cheap.

I eat more of the bread and cheese and pickle, open the bottle of liqueur, take a sip. The booze is regional, better than most—less sweet. I take a bigger sip.

I open the book by Likhachev, in which he recounts his arrival by ship on Great Solovetsky Island. He writes of being ordered by guards to help carry out the corpses of prisoners who had suffocated in the ship's hold. Then he was ordered to wash. "They led us, the living, to bathhouse No. 2. In the cold bathhouse they forced us to undress and took our clothes to be disinfected. We tested the water—only cold. About an hour later hot water appeared. In order to get warm I began to continuously pour hot water over myself. Finally they returned our clothes, smelling of sulfur. We got dressed."

Likhachev and the other prisoners had been deemed "enemies of the Revolution." Prior to their arrests, however, they were known simply as peasants and landowners, bureaucrats and aristocrats, anti-Communists and non-Communists, pagans and clergy, artists and scientists. "The great mixture of upper class and lower, of cleric and thief, of worker and scholar, created an oddly vital atmosphere in Solovki. One could labor side by side with princes or priests or prostitutes, in a democracy of convicts," American historian Roy Robson writes in his notable book, *Solovki.*

Some prisoners had been declared kulaks, peasants who owned more than the norm for the area in which they lived—a few cows, say, instead of one, or a house with a metal roof.

True criminals accounted for less than a third of all inmates on the Solovki.

Likhachev, like all new arrivals, was initially held in Transfiguration Cathedral—by then renamed No. 13 Company, a quarantine unit—where three stories of wooden shelves substituted for bunks for some 850 men. A dearth of windows, and ventilation, meant that a mist from sweat and wet clothing hung over the bunks, beneath which, Likhachev writes, the stone floor was "covered with a thick coating of dirt" and "heaps of decaying rubbish, shavings, and droppings of food," all of which "emitted a revolting stench."

Frescoes on the walls had been whitewashed. On the altar a portrait of Vladimir Lenin had been hung, beneath it the slogan: "Without education and cleanliness there is no road to socialism."

Likhachev returned to the archipelago in the 1960s, during the post-Stalin thaw ushered in by Soviet premier Nikita Khrushchev. A book Likhachev edited, *The Architectural-Artistic Monuments of the Solovetsky Islands*, relayed the poor condition of the infrastructure on Great Solovetsky, and suggested how it might be restored, inspiring a new kind of pilgrim to the island: young Soviets intent on fulfilling the plan.

Solzhenitsyn was stunned by the transformation. "Right now, there on the stones over which they dragged them, in that part of the courtyard secluded from the Solovetsky wind, cheerful tourists, who have come to see the notorious islands, *sock a volleyball* hours at a time. They do not know. Well, and if they did know? They would go on *socking* anyway."

Indeed, the travel brochure I picked up about the Solovki does not even mention the Gulag, but promotes the unique microclimate of the archipelago—which is somewhat sheltered from the Arctic by peninsulas and the White Sea, within which it sits in a sort of bay. The moisture and high salt content of the sea, at two tablespoons per quart, hold winter temperatures in check at around 13 degrees Fahrenheit. This means that the islands have hardwood and softwood trees—such as the snowball tree, and so-called "running trees" of stunted ash and birch slanted by persistent winds. The islands have wild roses, and wild mushrooms. They have hundreds of fresh-water lakes, and many kinds of fish. They have reindeer. They even have Beluga whales.

One of the islands even has ancient labyrinths—stones laid in shapes loosely resembling whirlpools—traced to peoples from between 2,000 and 3,000 BC.

There is much to see on the Solovki for outdoorsy types with only passing interest in the Gulag, and Russian Orthodoxy. One former inmate envisions a macabre tour for such visitors in his memoir, *Submergence into Darkness*. Oleg Volkov, who survived twenty-seven years in the Gulag, was invited back to the Solovki by acquaintances, but refused:

> The vanity of the tourists' exploratory venture struck me as insulting, even for my trifling ordeal. Ought I to have gone? To point out to my fellow travelers:

—Here agonized Musavatisty [members of a nationalist party in Azerbaijan in the early 1900s—b.m.].

—And here are buried bodies with bullet-riddled skulls.

—Not far from here in a building frame without a roof sat barefoot people in winter. Barefoot and in their underclothes. And in the summer months they were tied to stakes and eaten alive by mosquitoes.

—And here, along the shore, prisoners drew water from one hole in the ice and carried it, running, to pour into another hole in the ice. For hours, under the evil command, 'Scoop till it's dry!'

I close the Volkov, lean back against the outside wall of the shop. I am feeling drained from reading so much Russian, and from learning so much about injustices too recent to regard with the emotional cool of ancient history.

Solzhenitsyn and Volkov might as well have been writing about me: I came here from Arkhangelsk, my secular pilgrimage denied, merely to *be* this far north, on an isolated archipelago with a cool-sounding name. I *want* to know what it is like here to steam, to sweat deeply on the shores of Banya Lake, and to cool off in its waters under white skies at midnight. In the monastery I do not see evil, but a strange beauty.

In fact, the more I learn about the past on the islands, the longer I want to stay in this laboratory of unlikely coexistence.

It is interesting to be in a place where a new generation of monks and religious pilgrims are resuscitating the legacy of the hermitage founded by two ascetics more than five hundred years ago; where tourists paddle in boats along canals linking fifty-two lakes, stopping to pick berries and sniff flowers where the not-guilty slaved and died for the Soviet state; where seasonal laborers are giving new life, and purpose, to old structures built in the name of the Communist lie of labor as "the master of the world"; where all the while the words of those who suffered in our lifetimes grasp at the shirttails of a country sprinting to forget.

Gennady Andreev-Khomyakov, a former prisoner who, like Likhachev, served two terms on the Solovki, alludes to these tensions in his memoir, *Bitter Waters: Life and Work in Stalin's Russia*:

> The gloomy, moss-covered wall of the [monastery] presses into the earth like a gigantic iron. . . . Dark stones lie fixed, inviolable. . . . And you can't understand, you can't know, which stone was laid with a humble prayer, and which with a groan of despair. Which was wet with hot tears, and which was warmed with prayer. And where did the crack appear that gave way in our time to the precipice that turned this island into a place of continuous torment?

Streetlights flicker on overhead, their filaments a burnt orange against the white sky. I recall again the question posed to me by Father Gerasim: What is the *real* reason I have come here?

Back in the house my roommate has awakened. His name is Andrei, and he has traveled here, too, from Moscow. He tells me that he earns good money, but he does not say how, and I do not ask. His life works like this: "I sin. I fall into the gutter. I repent. I pull myself out of the mire, and then I do it all over again. . . . I try to spend less and less time in the mire." Andrei has been on the Solovki for two days, and he is lonely. He has decided to go home tomorrow even though he has yet to pray in Transfiguration Cathedral, to even set foot in the monastery.

I ask him to stay another day, to steam with me at the banya on Banya Lake. If he leaves now, I tell him, he will have spent more time on the train and boat he took to get here than on the island.

My treat, I say.

He shakes his head.

He wonders aloud why the short stories in his book are so bleak—even the Anton Chekhov, even the Ivan Bunin. He also wonders why I have yet to adopt Russian Orthodoxy, as it is no accident I have been living in Russia as long as I have.

The white curtains, doily-like, in the bedroom seem only to bring the white night closer. I want to sleep, but am not sure I can—because of the light, because of the snoring, because my mind is electric with new knowledge.

I am awakened, though, only by the landlady—who remembers about my banya reservation in the morning. She even has made me breakfast: cream of wheat with milk and fresh blueberries, and instant coffee, black, no sugar. I eat quickly, grab my flip-flops and Kyrgyz felt hat, walk outside.

A neighbor, Galya, is already waiting for me on the dirt road. She hands me a white plastic cup filled with small strawberries that grow among the potatoes and carrots in plots in the front and back yards of her house.

"Bitter, northern," she says.

Galya is short for Galina. She and her husband, Sasha—short for Aleksandr—own the most popular banya on the island. Locals call the banya either *Zaozyornaya*, the name of the muddy road off which it is situated, or, simply, The Banya of Sasha and Galya. It should be called The Banya of Galya and Sasha because Galya does all the work: she heats it, cleans it, and handles the money. Sasha, however, designed and built it.

The banya is small, compact, and resembles the tree forts of moneyed American children. It sits on a swamp filled in with dirt. It has a decorative well that yields brackish water; plans are afoot to build a plunge pool. "We dream about a bridge one day, too," Galya says, laughing, "something straight out of a fairytale."

She asks for money in advance: 250 rubles ($9.50) for two hours, fresh bundles of leafy birch included. Then she leads me into the banya, past two girls in their early twenties seated just outside the door, on a bench. Their eyes are closed. Their lips are closed in near smiles. The ends of their hair rest limp and wet on bare shoulders, the skin of which is pink and white and soft.

Inside Galya gestures to me wordlessly—toward the hooks on which to hang my clothes, the basin in which to soak my birch *veniki*, the basin with which to sluice my body with cool water. Then she leaves.

I undress, rinse off with cool water from a waist-high tank of rusting sheet metal. In the steam room some of the boards are black where, once upon a time, they briefly caught fire. The rocks on top of the stove are piled around a fat metal pipe through which water circulates, hot, from another rusted tank in the washroom.

The steam room is stuffy from the moist steam, the sweat, of the girls. I open the door, air it out; the steam room does not have a window, or a vent.

The temperature of the stove is not quite hot enough to allow me to make an intense steam; its heat is pleasant, enveloping, but unexceptional. I decide to steam long, not hard.

The most popular banya on Great Solovetsky Island is this one—The Banya of Sasha and Galya. The couple dreams of building a footbridge nearby, "something straight out of a fairytale."

I sit on the higher of two benches, knees up, back against a wall. I am alone, and alone with my thoughts. They are not deep.

Every handful of minutes I ladle hot water over the rocks. Sometimes I mix beer into the water, other times I dilute the water with mint or eucalyptus oils, splash the mixture against the tongue-and-groove planks on the walls and ceiling.

Between steams I drink two half-liter beers.

I steam six times over the two hours. When I leave the banya my heart is pounding, softly. Already two men are waiting on the bench outside.

I say hello. They say nothing.

My body feels loose in my clothes. I feel a lightness in my chest, and in my feet. I cannot bear putting on socks, damp and restrictive, so I am barefoot in my hiking boots.

I drop onto the bench. Breezes carry the scent of forests and water I cannot see. I call Father Gerasim on one of his cell phones. He agrees to show me the *bratskaya* banya the day after tomorrow, hangs up without saying goodbye.

I walk back to my room—to read and, maybe, to nap.

Andrei is gone. He has left me the book of bleak tales of religious inspiration.

I learn from the books I bought yesterday that there were at least four bathhouses at the labor camp. Two were located just outside the walls of the monastery; Likhachev washed in No. 2. A third sat at the bottom of a primitive stairwell on Mount Sekirna, one of two high hills on the island.

Known colloquially as Sekirka, the hill had two penal isolators—a logging camp at the base and, at the top, the Church of the Beheading of St. John the Baptist. In the church prisoners were often forced by guards to sit still for hours atop a pole. Many fell. Those who did were beaten. Others, ailing prisoners, were strapped to log beams and rolled down the 365 steps to their deaths.

The fourth bathhouse at the camp apparently is still standing. It is called Beletskaya, and it is located about a half mile from the monastery. A 1919 camp document dug up by Robson instructed guards to take prisoners to the village banya—Beletskaya was built in the 1700s—at least twice a month in order to stave off epidemics. A Kremlin-ordered review later found that guards ordered prisoners to walk there "absolutely naked, at twenty degrees below freezing."

The banya is two stories tall, and built in the style of the monastery: huge gray boulders at the base, red brick at the top. It is muscular, imposing. It is unlike any banya I have ever seen. I cannot steam in it because it is closed, indefinitely, for repairs.

Villagers earlier told me they steamed at Beletskaya until the late 1990s, when the municipal government built a new, particularly uninspired brick banya on Banya Lake. The new banya does not have an oven, but a boiler that delivers hot water through large pipes that maul the shoreline. It works only two days a week—once for men, once for women. At 350 rubles ($13) it is expensive, and the best

The massive Beletskaya banya—built in the 1700s in the style of the monastery, with boulders at the base and bricks at the top—is situated about a half mile from the monastery. During the Gulag inmates, "absolutely naked, at twenty degrees below freezing," were likely marched here, to wash.

assurance that the cheaper, more soulful Banya of Sasha and Galya will continue to be the island's most popular.

The other day I asked a secretary at the Solovetsky Historical and Architectural Museum-Preserve if she misses steaming at Beletskaya. "Yes, I have nostalgia," she told me. "There's always nostalgia for the past, good or bad—probably because it was something that no longer is."

The only account I can find of steaming in the camp is by Likhachev. Yet, as the prototype of the Gulag, bathhouses at SLON would have been much like those elsewhere—such as the Kolyma camp system so thoroughly documented by Shalamov in *Kolyma Tales*:

> The banya is always a negative event, a burden in the life of prisoners. One would think, how could this be? . . . What's going on? Could it be that a person, no matter how deep he has been driven to misery,

refuses to wash in a banya—to rinse from himself the dirt and sweat that covers his body, festering with skin diseases, and feel cleaner if only for an hour?

There's a Russian proverb: "Happy, as if fresh from the banya." The saying is accurate, and reflects precisely the physical bliss a person with a clean, scrubbed body experiences. Can it be true that the common sense of people has been lost to such a degree that they don't understand, don't want to understand, that it's better without lice, than with lice?

In Kolyma prisoners were given an hour to undress, wash, and dress. A hundred men could be forced into space intended for fifteen—chilled, nonetheless, by drafts from doorways and cracks in walls. Outer garments, as well as dirty underwear, were collected and steamed separately in an effort to kill lice.

Each prisoner was given a pail of scalding hot water, which he cooled with chunks of ice that stuck to the fingers. While he washed, his valuable scraps of clothing—spare mittens, foot rags—were likely to be stolen.

After washing, Shalamov writes, men gathered outside a small dark window in the bathhouse to receive disinfected underwear. As soon as the board to the window was raised, they shouldered against each other with "slippery, dirty, stinking bodies" to claim underwear that, often, was still wet. Shalamov says it is "strange and painful to the point of tears" to watch adult men cry after receiving clean worn-out underwear in exchange for dirty good underwear. "Nothing can compel a person to turn away from the hardships that comprise life," he writes. "Not even the blatant realization that it's merely one bath, whereas, in the end, it's his life that's been lost."

The bath scene in Dostoevsky's novel, *Notes from the Dead House*, was written nearly a century earlier, yet has much in common with Shalamov's stories. Dostoevsky, too, had been imprisoned—for four years, in Siberia—for his role in a secret group that opposed serfdom and autocracy under the tsars. In the book he writes about the lives of convicts in a Siberian prison through a narrator, the gentleman inmate Aleksandr Petrovich Goryanchikov. In chapter nine Goryanchikov learns how to undress, wash and dress in leg irons: "When we opened the door to the banya itself, I thought that we had walked into Hell. Imagine a room twelve paces long and just as wide into which maybe upwards of one hundred people—at least eighty, probably—had been crammed all at once. . . . Steam that clouded the eyes, soot, grime, so crowded that there was no place to put your foot. I got scared and wanted to turn back."

Each man was given a pail of hot water and a piece of soap the size of a two-kopeck coin. Goryanchikov held the fetters around his calves so as not to fall as he searched for a place to stand, and wash. (Space to sit, like extra soap, could be bought.) Some men resorted to squatting under benches, where "sticky moisture had built up everywhere to a depth of nearly half a finger." "Filthy water dripped . . . directly onto the shaven heads of those seated beneath" other men who washed, standing. He continues:

> On the bench and all the steps leading up to it sat bathers, squatting and hunched up together. But they barely washed. Common people wash little with hot water and soap; they merely steam hard, then rinse off with cold water—that's their entire bath. All along the bench fifty *veniki* rose and fell at once, everyone beat themselves to point of intoxication. More steam was made by the minute. It was no longer simply burning, it was scorching. The whole banya roared with yelling and laughter, accompanied by the sound of one hundred chains dragging across the floor . . .
>
> Dirt streamed down from all sides. Everyone was in some kind of drunken, some kind of excited state; screams and cries rang out . . . The shaven heads and steamed red bodies of the prisoners seemed even more hideous. The scars from past blows with whips and rods stand out unusually clear on a freshly steamed back, so much so that all the backs seemed injured anew. Terrible scars! A shiver ran across my skin just looking at them. Then they throw more water into the stove and the steam covers the entire banya in a dense, hot cloud; everyone begins to hoot and holler. From the cloud of steam flash battered backs, shaven heads and gnarled arms and legs.
>
> It struck me that if one day we all should wind up together in hell's corner, it would be very much like this place.

People often liken the infernal heat of the steam room to Hell. It is a natural, if sometimes easy, simile. To me, though, the banya has never been hellish, only heavenly.

Father Gerasim said that *Notes from the Dead House* would help me understand the Russian soul. I wonder what he thinks the book says about Russia, not to mention its soul?

In my room I am tired from steaming, and from reading. Throughout the afternoon I nap, read, nap some more, read some more. When I can read, and sleep, no longer, I walk to the local cafeteria, eat two small salads (seaweed, and pickled cabbage with green apples and red bog berries) and a bowl of fish soup with dark bread. Then I walk off the meal, walk to the old hotel, where I book tours of the labyrinths and the former Gulag.

From the hotel I stray off the road onto a sandy trail that I follow around shallow lakes, through groves of unpretentious birch, and across waterlogged terrain held in place by the roots of green and yellow grasses. I am still disoriented from all that I have read and, I think, the white of the sky—which seems to be disrupting my body's natural rhythms.

How does one know when to end anything when the skies always portend something new?

The breezes harden, flatten, as I walk. They are strong enough to keep mosquitoes from alighting on my skin. Around me large wooden crosses, along the trail and in the distances, rise intermittently from wooden pedestals similar to decorative planters filled with rock. Broad planks rest on the arms of the crosses and meet at the peaks, forming a sort of roof.

The trail stops at a beach of hard sand cluttered with rocks and uncommonly large driftwood. Tangled strands of dark yellow seaweed jostle softly in the White Sea shallows. I dip a hand in the water, taste its salt on my fingers.

For a second straight night I sleep well, almost oversleep the tours of the labyrinths, the Gulag. Exhibits at the museum are clear-eyed, and terrific; the narratives on the placards are so honest I almost cannot believe that today's Kremlin has not shuttered the museum for oft-cited technical reasons.

I learn from the tour guide, Yulia, a college student from the

Crosses like this are scattered across the open territory of Great Solovetsky Island.

mainland, that bathhouses in the camp were a rough-edged pleasure: prisoners were given clean shirts after washing, yet forced to
stand outdoors, irrespective of the weather, for lengthy periods. Often, she says, the shirts had been on the backs of other prisoners
only hours before—as evidenced by bullet holes in the fabric.

"To this day the banya is remembered as a wonderful place where
prisoners could warm up, get rid of dirt, and put on clean clothes,"
Yulia says.

Likhachev and Shalamov would say otherwise.

I book time at the banya on Banya Lake and, in mid-evening, arrive alone. Locals call it the Fedotovskaya Banya, after the owner's
surname, Fedotov. I sit on a small bench next to a metal barbeque,
wait for the owner to arrive with the key.

The pine siding is silvery in the light.

"You're lucky," the owner, Elena, tells me.

The only reason she was able to meet me, she says, is that she
could not convince her husband, who is overworked managing

their chain of seven hardware stores, to go fishing overnight.

Elena is petite, naturally pretty. I wonder if she has a younger sister.

She also tells me that, the other day, she began to catch a cold, so she steamed in the banya—doused herself with cold and hot water—and it went away.

I wonder if, perhaps, she would like to take a lover.

"This is our first banya," she says. "As is typical for first banyas, it's unfinished."

The banya is built from pine boards, but Elena would have preferred ash. The stove is stoked primarily with pine, too, but Elena would have preferred birch; birch costs more, she says, but it burns longer and lends "spirit" to the steam.

At least the bundles of leafy twigs are birch. Still, Elena would have preferred ashberry, which she says "brings forth abundance, and beauty."

For any banya, though, the stove is a revelation: it was designed and built by engineers who design and build nuclear submarines in nearby Severodvinsk. It heats the spacious steam room to some 212 degrees Fahrenheit in less than two hours.

No one else has booked time this evening, so Elena offers me a deal: 1,000 rubles ($37.50) for four hours, a 600-ruble savings. I pay Elena for four hours. She leaves when her son, Igor, arrives on a bicycle to stoke the stove.

Igor is fifteen, but he looks twelve. He is thin like a girl is willowy. His black and white sweater smells of smoke. Igor initially uses pine, but generously finishes stoking the stove with birch after conjuring several logs, the bark of which is green with lichen. He, too, leaves.

I undress quickly, hang my clothes on pegs in the lounge next to wall hangings of a cartoon man and woman—naked, with strategically placed bundles of leafy birch twigs—beneath the sayings, "How well you steamed is how well you recuperated," and "In the banya, a *venik* is worth more than money."

In the washroom the planks on the walls are streaked with black from corroding nails. Some boards are mildewed. I fill a tub with cool water and submerge the leafy tops of two bundles of birch, included in the price. I open the door to the steam room, duck beneath the transom, pull shut the door.

Perhaps the best banya on the Solovki is this one, Fedotovskaya, which sits on the shore of a small lake in which bathers cool between steams. Certainly the steam room has the most powerful stove: it was built by engineers who design nuclear submarines.

Unlike the heat yesterday at The Banya of Sasha and Galya, temperatures at Fedotovskaya are strong enough to let me manipulate the steam—to dial it down, or dial it up—to suit my moods. I will steam hard, tonight.

Still, I start slow. I mix beer with hot water and drizzle it over the rocks in the stove. I am impatient to smell the scent of the beer, so I place a thumb over the mouth of the bottle, shake it twice, spray foam lightly over the metal.

I duck back into the washroom, massage into my already sweaty skin granules of salt extracted from White Sea seaweed. My armpits, and the areas behind my knees, begin to tingle. Then I return to the steam room, add peppermint oil to a ladle of water, and splash it against the walls.

The mint does not complement, but overwhelms, the beer. I am overeager.

Over the next hour or so I take breaks frequently—cool off under basins of water in the washroom, relax in the lounge. Between
steams I drink mineral water, and hot tea. The tea is a blend con-
cocted by Elena: dried leaves of black bilberry, black currant, whor-
tleberry, and raspberry commingled with an English breakfast tea.
To brew it I drop fingerfuls of loose tea into a kettle, then fill the
kettle with hot water from a chrome-plated samovar, steam from
which condenses on the glass panes of a window.

The flier on the cement telephone pole advertised a steam room
that reaches temperatures of 212 degrees. The closest I can get,
though, is 209 degrees. Still, at that temperature, even a lighter, drier
steam burns the insides of my nostrils, my throat.

I cover my mouth and nose with a gloved hand as the 209-degree
steam settles from the ceiling over my body—a process I feel first on
my eyelids, then behind my ears, then along my back, and then on
the tops of my thighs. I use the other gloved hand to cover my penis.

Afterward, while cooling in the washroom, I notice in a mirror
spots of white pus at the inside corners of my eyes. I decide that the
pus is either a by-product of toxins that have left my body, or a soft
mucousy layer of something, or other, that has been singed.

I put on my green boxer shorts and walk outside, along the narrow wooden pier that reaches into Banya Lake. To one side, in the
water, is a rusted oil barrel. To the other is a thin rusted pipe that
leads, seemingly, to nowhere.

Bugs, gnats and mosquitoes, swarm above the water. White but-
terflies flit among them, unsure. The water is the color of tea, and
smells of minerals. It is effervescent, really—very nearly bubbly.
Clumps of soft, airy, dark green algae float on top, like offal.

I jump in, feet first.

I am treading water when the tips of my toes brush bottom—or,
rather, sweep through a cool, airy layer (decaying leaves, I hope).
The sensation makes me squeamish. Instantly I envision skulls,
bones of former prisoners who drowned here, or whose bodies
were simply dumped.

I kick out, flatten my body along the surface of the lake and swim
overhand, head above water, to the pier.

Inside the banya I rinse off, duck into the steam room. I lie on my back on the uppermost of two benches. This time I do not add any-thing, any scents, to the steam, for I am already overcome by waves of good feeling that sometimes take minutes, sometimes hours—and sometimes never come. The waves seem to emanate from the center of my body, just behind the diaphragm. They travel to the tips of my toes and fingers, where they strain against my skin in pleasant throbs.

I wish I were not alone. From the lounge I send text messages to the cell phones of friends with whom I steam in Moscow.

One, an Italian, writes back, "We're with you, mate."

I decide to end my last steam by counting, slowly, to one hundred. I stop at seventy-seven: I already hit my high, the steam is very hot, and seventy-seven is a good number, the product of two primes.

I stop counting, actually, about the time I am wondering why I am leaving Russia for the United States, where I cannot recall the last time I felt this alive.

It is around midnight when Igor returns. I thank him for using the birch, wish him "with light steam" as we wave goodbye.

Outside the sky is a dirty, bright white. It begins to spit rain as I make my way along the slow twists of the sandy road. I put on my skullcap, pull it low enough to cover my ears, my eyebrows—offer the mosquitoes only my lips and nose.

I will not smear repellent on my clean, clean skin.

My legs are tired, as if I have done too many squats with a heavy weight. I walk past the intimidating Beletskaya banya, past a former agar works, up a small incline, past a monument to World War II dead in which a family of finches has made a nest, up a sudden incline, then past the old hotel, down a hill, along the bay, past the monastery, past the carcass of the hydroelectric station, past the lake, past the bus-cum-bookstore, and into the grocery shop, where I buy a bottle of fresh kefir for breakfast.

Then I go into the café without a name, where I drink two shots of red bog-berry liqueur.

Before falling asleep I decide that, if there is a spot on tomorrow's flight to the mainland, I will take it.

The next morning I drop by the monastery on the way to the air-field, the landing strip of which is comprised of sections of sheet metal linked, side-by-side, just long (and wide) enough for a small plane to take off, and touch down.

Father Gerasim greets me on the same plot of trampled grass. In his robe of faded black I am reminded of the most devout Solovki monks who wore robes embroidered with skulls and bones to symbolize being dead to earthly cares.

Father Gerasim is quiet, pensive. I feel as if I am imposing upon him. He walks to the far end of the dormitory. I follow. He opens a heavy wooden door, points me inside—into the *bratskaya* banya.

Just past the door quartered logs of birch are stacked in square columns in an anteroom that leads into a long room of red brick with vaulted ceilings. At the far end of the room is an extremely narrow steam room, the walls of which are paneled in pine. I begin taking photographs.

"I hope I didn't offend you the other day," Father Gerasim says, using the formal *Vy* instead of *ty*.

No, I say. How could you have offended me?

"I don't know."

We sit down. I tell him that if he felt any tension, any unease, it more than likely stemmed from me and my opinion of the Church— an opinion that does not apply to the majority of its adherents.

We are quiet. We utter clipped thoughts. We are trying to be honest, but do not yet understand what we are feeling.

I finish taking notes, photos. I am relieved when Father Gerasim ushers me outside, into the courtyard.

"You like smoked fish? With beer, probably?" he says.

Sure, I tell him. Even without beer.

"Here. Try this."

He reaches into his robes and brings out a fish rolled tightly in newspaper. "You've never had fish like this before," he says.

I am reluctant to take it. It's a local fish?

"Yeah."

You can get it all the time?

"Yeah."

So, like, you have a lot of it?

"Yeah."

Really?

Water from these hand-welded tanks is heated as it circulates through a pipe that wends among rocks in the floor-to-ceiling stove of the monks' banya.

"To the brim!"

Alright then. I thank him.

Father Gerasim hands me the fish. Again he reaches into his robes and, with a small, intentional flourish, hands me an icon about three inches by two inches. It is a replica of a Byzantine icon, a solemn, thin-faced Jesus gesticulating with the fingers on his right hand. The icon is flecked with 24- and 18-karat gold.

"This is for you, so God protects you," Father Gerasim says. "I want you to know that you always have a place here."

I am sincerely touched. I resolve to buy and mail him a book of reproductions of the works of Andrew Wyeth, his favorite painter, when I return to the States.

I thank him again, turn to leave.

"By the way ..."

I stop, look back.

Plastic basins await the next Saturday, when the monks typically steam in their bunker-like banya. One monk makes the steam for everyone else. Older, more venerated monks steam first.

"It's about time you got married."
He smiles. I smile, too.
He had referred to me as *ty*.

The Banya Is Life
«Баня—это жизнь»

We would be resting between steams, our hair wet, our skin flushed, our backs slumped against benches, our chests rising and falling with a slow, pleasant fatigue from swings in temperature, hot to cold to hot to cold.

We would talk about our jobs, and our loves. We would talk about ourselves, too, when we were able to see ourselves as independent from work, or women.

Sometimes we would talk about what we were feeling, not emotions so much as the physical sensations common to our chosen bathhouse in Moscow. Was the steam dry enough, soft enough, light enough? Were our senses aroused more, say, by the aroma of beer with reassuring overtones of mustard, or that of wormwood with slashing accents of peppermint?

Sometimes, when the steam was just right, we would not talk at all. Great steam, like great art, has the power to bring on quiet.

Such moments, for me, were a rejuvenating confluence of communion. With myself. With others. With the divine. Every so often, though, these spells of good feeling would be broken by declarations from other bathers, always Russian, that what we were experiencing, in fact, was not special.

"You call this a banya? This isn't a banya, this isn't a banya. There is only one true banya, one true *Russian* banya—the *black* banya!"

"The steam here is good. I won't dispute that, I won't. But you'll never know what steam truly is until you've steamed in a *real* Russian banya, till you've steamed *black-style!*"

Most of it was hearsay, I knew. More Russians have seen the yeti than have steamed in a black banya.

Black banyas are nearly extinct. They just barely exist. They are the truest link to the ancient Slavic steam baths of another millennium.

Black banyas are black because they do not have chimneys. Literally, they are black: the ceiling and interior walls are caked with soot, from smoke.

I have never appreciated being ripped out of a moment by someone telling me that there was a better moment, elsewhere, to be had. Over time, though, the remarks of other bathers caused the vision in my mind of a dingy, soot-encrusted black banya to shimmer with the enchanting sheen of myth. Over time, I came to regard my appreciation for the Russian cult of steam a bit like Cicero regarded his history: "Not to know what happened before one was born is always to be a child."

Knowledge and awareness are not peers of experience; like the dismissive remarks of the other bathers, they are only so much hearsay.

I decided to find a black banya, and to steam in it.

I began my search by tracing my footsteps as a reporter. I had seen black banyas in Russia, but they were long dormant, relocated from villages to open-air museums of wooden architecture in the Far North (on the island of Kizhi, and at *Malye Korely*, on the hills outside Arkhangelsk). I probably had seen black banyas in far-flung villages, too, only I did not recognize them for what they were, because I was not sure what they were. These banyas without chimneys resemble dilapidated sheds, or huts. Their walls of logs or clapboard often slant, all but fall into themselves. Their roofs tend to be patched with whatever materials were at hand; sometimes the ceilings are merely sprinkled from above with soil, from which sprout grasses and wildflowers. Their floors of dirt, or rough-hewn planks, often are strewn with straw.

At best these banyas are prototypes of a simple peasant cottage with a low door, a small window, and two small rooms—one in which to steam, and another in which to wash.

I searched the Russian-language Internet, delved into databases of provincial newspapers and magazines. I posted messages to online banya forums. I simply asked around.

"It'll be difficult, it'll be difficult to find one," a Russian friend told me. He said he knew of an old black banya outside Moscow whose door was so small, so low to the ground, that one had to crawl through it, supplicant.

Too bad, he said, it had been torn down some months back.

"This kind of thing is happening all over Russia. These banyas should be put in museums before it's too late."

The banya about which he spoke might very well have outlived two empires: the Russian empire, which was conquered by the Bolsheviks in 1917, and the Soviet empire, which effectively conquered itself in 1991. But the banya did not outlive the nascent years of the Russian Federation, in which steaming black-style is out of favor, museums barely have enough money for utilities, and cultural landmarks stand little chance against the will of those with a stake in the business of tearing down, and building up.

That is one of the ironies of this new, yet not-so-new country—for the terrain of daily life here is dotted with standing pools of longing, of nostalgia, for what once was, but is lost.

Deceased Soviet leaders. Transcendent Soviet artists and cultural icons. The innocence and certitude of childhoods lived behind the Iron Curtain. Achievements on the battlefield, and in outer space. Feelings of power and respect and relevance in the world. These pools of nostalgia are regenerative for a great many people who ache to feel good about themselves, and their country, after many years, when they did not. They symbolize the stability of a tradition, something Lewis Hyde, the American poet, says has "its roots not only in a historical or cultural past, but within the innermost being of man."

And therein lies the irony. Elements of culture that are essential to the country's sense of place, to its sense of self—indeed, to its very notion of a national soul—are disappearing with a nod to the few, and not the many.

Certainly it is happening with the black banya, the great-granddaddy of the banya.

And the banya is the most Russian thing there is.

This is all for the best, according to another Russian friend. He can withstand the hottest temperatures in the steam room longer than anyone I have ever seen. More impressively, he can do so while slurring his speech, still buzzed from the previous night's party. "Don't believe everything they tell you about the black banya," he once told me, while sober. "A black banya simply is a bad banya, a poor banya."

His remarks speak to things like comfort, design, and safety. They do not speak to that which he cannot quantify: the essence of steam, its spirit.

It is not wrong to speak of steam possessing a spirit. Each steam room has its own vibe, its own mood; we like the steam in some banyas, we like the steam less in others.

For centuries Russian folklore has spoken of the bathhouse possessing a spirit. More to the point, the bathhouse is possessed by a spirit. For a bathhouse can look empty in Russia, but it never is. It is said to be home to the most powerful of the country's legion of domestic goblins, the aforementioned *bannik*.

The *bannik* is a disembodied spirit. Sometimes it is said to assume the form of a snake or a black cat, a black dog. Sometimes it is said to appear as a small old man, naked, with a big head, shaggy hair, spindly limbs, and a molting green beard.

Sometimes the *bannik* is not seen, but heard—in the rustle of leaves from a bundle of birch twigs, or as a voice in the dark, snoring, whistling, laughing, howling. The spirit is said to be felt, too— in the grope of a paw, the claws only just retracted, or that of a cold, hairy, heavily knuckled hand down a bare spine.

The *bannik* (also *baennik*) is a pagan deity that was demonized after Russia adopted Christianity in the tenth century. In some regions it is said to be one of the rebellious angels driven out of heaven by Michael the Archangel. In others it is said to have been born of a fight between God and the Devil in a bathhouse.

In most of the tales passed down in the oral tradition of Russian storytelling, however, the disposition of the goblin of the bathhouse is not so absolute. Just as the banya is seen to straddle the natural and unnatural worlds, the loyalties of the *bannik*, too, are split.

"There are no evil *banniki*, but there are no kind ones, either," goes a proverb in the Far North.

There are other reputed haunts of evil forces in Russia—crossroads, thresholds, holes in the ice over a lake, or river. All of these places can "clearly be seen to be liminal areas at which a magical other world begins," writes Ryan in *The Bathhouse at Midnight*.

But none is transcendent like a village banya, at midnight.

"It is unclear: is [the banya] a building or, perhaps, a living thing?

Or is it a secret abode, inhabited by creatures who reside in another dimension and only rarely show their faces to people?" writes Neonila A. Krinichna, a folklorist from the Far North.

No one talks of the *bannik* in big-city bathhouses, the places I usually steam. Its presence is more apt to be associated with bathhouses that accommodate a few, not dozens.

Perhaps that is inevitable in a megalopolis like Moscow, which Muscovites like to call "a country within a country." They are referring to the pace, to the disproportionate volumes of people, power, and money. The banya is important to life in the city, but it is not essential for living. (That is the case, anyway, for all but three weeks in spring, when the government denies hot water to residents while workers ostensibly perform maintenance on the Soviet-era water and sewerage systems.)

In fact, the scope with which urban bathhouses have strained from their roots can be seen at an elite banya complex where the city's lone black banya, of recent construction, is displayed like a rare animal at a zoo. It is not there for the merely curious, but for the well-heeled: it costs 6,000 rubles per hour, or $240, to use it.

But "Moscow is not Russia," as Muscovites are fond of saying. For this, I am grateful. If my friend is right, and a black banya is a poor banya, I will need to travel where people live poorly in order to find one. Perhaps only there I will find a history that is at once ancient, and alive.

I had narrowed my search to a splash of territory in northwestern Siberia when an e-mail dropped into my inbox with a virtual kerplunk.

"Hi! I want to do present for you. I think I can organize a real black banya for you. I spoke with my cousin. She is your age. Even both your birthdays are in March. You can stay at her place. They are very simple people. She promised to organize a black banya for you. Those kinds of banyas no one, nowhere, do anymore. But you need to travel to Chuvashiya. It is not far. I will explain everything. They will meet you. If you want to, of course . . . ? Later, Nataliya."

She got that from me, the "later" part—that and the gratuitous ellipses. Nataliya is a longtime friend to whom I have been giving crash courses in English to help her prepare for a job interview. I teach my native language the same way I taught myself Russian: I begin by instilling enough words, and enough confidence, to give the illusion of deep knowledge. That is all she needs, for now.

Nataliya was born and raised in Chuvashiya, a semi-autonomous republic of black earth and rolling hills in the Volga River basin. On a map the republic looks to be in the country's midwest, but, to most Russians, Chuvashiya is the south.

I had not thought about points south in my search for a black banya. In the south, people historically have steamed less in bath-houses, and more in the large ovens that squat in the common rooms of traditional peasant cottages, or *izbi*.

Such ovens are simply called Russian ovens, or *Russkiye pechki*. They are no-way-they-make-ovens-that-big-what-for-that's-silly-I-don't-believe-it large. Typically they are longer and wider than the bed of a pick-up truck, and nearly as tall as the roof of the cab. They are made of brick, or clay. Usually they are plastered smooth then whitewashed.

Russian ovens are so big that, one winter, I slept on top of one—in the space between the oven and the ceiling—in the log cabin in which I was living, alone, in a nearly abandoned village outside Moscow. I had moved to Meshchery in a bid to place myself far from that which tempted me to distraction, things like girls, party-ing, and, even, friends.

Alone and anonymous, I thought, I would have little choice but to write.

The oven, like all Russian ovens, was designed not only to cook food, but to radiate heat. Only my oven was old, and did not retain heat for long: one morning I awoke to temperatures of 21 degrees Fahrenheit, indoors. So, on nights when temperatures outdoors fell to *minus* 21 degrees Fahrenheit, I slept on a thin cotton mattress that I heaved on top of a pallet on the oven.

It helped that, on some of those nights, I shared the space above the oven with a lover, a gifted language student from Sweden. She would arrive, unannounced, after slogging some twenty-five minutes through thigh-high snow from the train platform in a nearby village. I never knew if her visits spoke more of her feelings for me, or the intrepid nature of Swedish women.

That winter I washed in an old banya in the yard. It did not occur to me to scoop out the coals from the Russian oven, shed my clothes, and shimmy, feet first, into the warm, dark hollow. That might have been because, in the old banya, I sometimes steamed with my lover—once, even, with her girlfriends, three Swedes and a Finn. More likely, though, it was because the inside of the Russian oven was dusted with ash, poorly ventilated, and cramped; my shoulders are naturally broad, and the opening was narrow.

For centuries, though, Russian ovens were more popular than bathhouses in the south, and even in some parts of the north. Sometimes it was a matter of cost: bathhouses require extra wood to build, and to heat, and wood can be scarce in regions dominated by steppe or swamp. Sometimes it was a matter of convenience: banyas take time to heat, and families already had Russian ovens that they used every day for cooking. (Moreover, children could be picked up and placed inside an oven, and the elderly and infirm could be slid inside on a wooden peel.)

Surely someone, somewhere, continues to steam in his Russian oven. But the practice effectively died out by the 1930s, around the same time, not coincidentally, that the Soviet government was actively building public bathhouses for all.

A friend's father, a banya enthusiast in Nizhny Novgorod, recently built a Russian oven simply to feel what it is like to steam, within. For me, the allure fell away when I considered that, throughout much of the country's history, Russian ovens were the centerpieces of houses that did not have chimneys—houses in which people slept above the oven, or on narrow wooden benches along the walls, while their animals slept, and defecated, on the dirt floor.

I have come closest to experiencing what it is like to steam in a Russian oven by reading the accounts of others, such as N. Preobrazhensky, who chronicled a visit with relatives in the northwestern territory of Vologda over New Year's in 1860. Librarians and academics are unsure, but Preobrazhensky is likely the Nikolai Sergeevich Preobrazhensky known to be a friend of the noted critic, Nikolai Dobrolyubov, and described by a contemporary as possessing a high opinion of himself, untrammeled judgment, and a unique appearance: "short of stature, long nose and hair standing on end like a bird's crest."

Preobrazhensky had assumed that everyone steamed in bathhouses. So when an uncle suggested steaming, the author sat down in the house to wait for the older man to get ready. He watched as a maid carried in an armful of straw, then swung open the metal door of the oven, which was still warm from cooking, and scattered the straw over the bottom of the hollow. She picked up a basin of warm water, in which a bundle of leafy birch twigs already was soaking, and placed the basin inside. She shut the door.

> A short time later my uncle appeared, naked, in the middle of the cottage. He rubbed his beard and, without saying a word, marched into the oven after the straw, the basin and the bundle of leafy twigs. The cottage did not have any [interior] walls, therefore, everyone could see what was happening from all angles. The maid closed the hatch to the oven. I thought that my uncle was thinking of making a roast of himself, but that wasn't the case. Indeed, from inside the stove—where they cook cabbage soup and porridge, bake bread, pies and other rich things, and into which crawled my beloved relative—could be heard powerful slaps, moans, groans, one-syllable exclamations and entire words of approval, such as, "Grand!," "Nice!," "Glorious!," "Well, well!," "I say!," "Ahh!," "And again, again!," "Ooh, how grand!"
>
> That was my uncle whipping himself, so that he had strength all over, like a sexton. Two, three times the water gurgled. A muffled cry could be heard: "Open up!" The maid opened the oven and my uncle, red all over, like a boiled crayfish, crawled out head first. Again he stuck his head and beard into the oven, took out the basin with the bundle of leafy twigs, and, resembling Adam in a state of innocence, walked the length of the cottage before turning in to the cellar to pour cold water over himself.

I am content to read about steaming in a Russian oven, but I am not content to merely read about steaming in a black banya. So when Nataliya offers to arrange for me to steam black-style, or *pochyornomu*, I agree without hesitation—even though I am not at all certain where Chuvashiya is, on a map. I call Nataliya's cousin, Maria. All I need to do, she says, is hop on a train that stops in the small town of Vurnary, some 650 miles away. She and her husband, Gennady, will meet me at the station.

I am feeling anxious when I pack an overnight bag with my clothes, flip-flops, and banya hat. I am accustomed to feeling this way before a trip, almost any trip; sometimes I even feel nauseous. These feelings can last from a few hours to most of the day. They just happen. I cannot control them. I long have stopped trying to figure out why.

Certainly the anxiety is gone by the time I arrive, by subway, at the city's Kazansky Train Station. I did not notice it leave.

In the station I buy a one-way ticket, look up at the split-flap display of times and destinations. I make my way up stairs, down escalators, through doors, and along underground walkways, to the trains.

I am still carrying my bag, but already I feel lighter. I have yet to leave Moscow, but I am only barely here. I am in a sort of neutral territory from which the past seems clearly behind, and the future seems literally ahead. I am about to go somewhere I have never been, a place with a cool-sounding name, where I am about to do something I have never done, something no one I know has ever done.

The older I get, the more I value first times. For anything.

The air outside is cold on my face, enlivening. The vaguely metallic scent of burning coal settles high in my nostrils.

About a dozen passenger trains are stopped, staggered, along cement platforms. I find my train and walk toward it with long, steady strides past the police officers in gray, submachine guns slung over their shoulders. My expression is one of practiced blankness, of an indifference toward the police, who are looking to stop anyone who stands out, typically those with darker skin.

My train is long. I walk past the caboose, about a dozen sleeper cars, the restaurant car, and another dozen sleeper cars before I reach mine, number twenty-six. My body is warm, my shirt clingy from sweat. I set down my bag on end. It is a custom in Russia to sit on one's suitcase, to be quiet, before a trip. I cannot sit on my bag; it is soft, fabric stitched around a backpack frame.

I place a hand on it, instead. My mind already is quiet.

I watch as passengers stand in lines, askew. Women stay with bags as men suck hard on cigarettes and move to flick the butts, still smoldering, into the dark space between the train and the platform. They approach the conductor, a middle-aged woman in a long dark coat, woolen stockings, low heels, and a small-billed cap. She compares the names on tickets to the names on domestic passports, then hands back the documents while pronouncing the number of the compartment, and bunk.

Others—relatives, friends, lovers—accompany passengers inside. It is important in Russia to do this, to *provozhat'*. If, at an airport, only passengers can get beyond checkpoints, at a train station in Russia anyone can accompany someone to a car and sit on a bunk until moments before the wheels begin to roll.

No one, ever, escorts me to a train. Not anymore. Years ago, when I first moved here, Russians were worried about me and made sure I got on trains safely. Occasionally girlfriends accompanied me, too. One, a young divorcee of Georgian descent, presented me with a pastry of light dough layered heavy with a salty cheese, the heat of which I held in my palms while I beheld a different heat, hers, on my lips.

The sweat on my skin has begun to cool. I hoist my bag, get in line. I hand the conductor the card that says I am accredited as a journalist with the Ministry of Foreign Affairs. It has my photo, a stamp, and a signature. It is in Russian. She glances at the card, gives it back. Then she asks for my passport, which is in English. She flips through the pages, looks at all the visas and stamps, because she can.

She hands me back my ticket and passport, holds out an arm toward the open door of the car. "Please," she says.

I shuffle sideways along the corridor, which is wide enough for a man, but not a man and his luggage. My compartment is crowded. I excuse myself, step around one person, past another, and heft my bag onto an upper bunk. I walk out. In the corridor I stop before a window. Strangers are waving in my direction.

"Two minutes, two minutes!"

The conductor is negotiating her way along the corridor, her chin lifted as if to cast her words above the arc of noise—conversation, laughter, the broadcast of a popular radio station, Evropa-Plus.

A deejay is telling a joke:

> An Armenian fills out a visa application at a consulate. Where it says sex, he writes, proudly, "Three times a day."
> Where it says man or woman, he writes, "Makes no difference."

"We are leaving, we are leaving," the conductor says. "The train is leaving."

The car jerks forward, stops. It is as if the engineer is saying, really, she means it.

People brush against my back, wordless, on their ways out. I return to my compartment. On a lower bunk sits a man in his twenties with close-cropped hair and a black T-shirt, the word, РОССИЯ, in white block letters across the shoulder blades. On the other bunk sit a young woman and a young boy. The young woman has skin the color of light caramel. She is not wearing any makeup. She is beautiful.

Good evening, I say. I sit down next to the young man.

Above us are upper bunks. Between us is a pop-up table with a tablecloth of rough linen upon which sit a large bottle of mineral water, a package of crackers, a small tin of processed meat, a small rectangle of cheese, two apples, and a pear.

One of the most well-known songs in the country, "Touch by Touch," spills out from speakers in the ceiling. It is by Joy, an Austrian pop trio from the eighties that sang in English.

> When my heart is full of love
> It makes me a turtledove
> Love's a game that we play
> Night and day
>
> When our love is clear and bright
> It's our way to see the light
> There's a fire in our hearts
> Night and day

I ask the girl her name.

"Tamara," she says. "And you?"

I tell her. I ask if the boy is her son.

"Five," she says. "Gena."

The name is short for Gennady.

"He has more paperwork than I do."

Tamara is petite and slim with a voluptuous chest that I did not notice, at first, beneath a loose T-shirt of faded green. Her teeth are white, and her smile is cartoon perfect.

"You have very good Russian," she says.

It is still early, I say. Soon my store of vocabulary words will run out.

She laughs. "For some reason I doubt that."

I cannot meet her smile. The corners of my mouth feel heavy. My smile, I realize, has too far to travel to arrive appropriate to the moment. I smile with my eyes.

The wheels of the train begin to roll, slowly.

> Do it, we still do it night and day
> You're my all time lover
> Do it, we still do it in a way
> Like there is no other
>
> Touch by touch
> You're my all time lover
> Skin to skin
> Come under my cover.

The conductor walks in, sits next to the boy, sighs. She collects our tickets, rolls them up, slips them into pockets in a notebook. Tamara and Gena have the upper bunks. I look up; the bunks do not have safety rails. It is a long way to fall for a five-year-old boy.

The conductor closes the notebook, gets up to leave. "Will anyone be having tea, coffee? Perhaps the boy would like some cookies?"

I'd like some tea, I say. Lemon, no sugar.

"Five rubles," she says. "You'll have to wait."

I do not really want the tea as much as I want to cup its heat in my hands. I also want to see how the tea is served, whether it will arrive in a ceramic mug or a glass that nests inside an elaborate holder, usually burnished metal with a handle. Some railway lines have their own designs.

I offer my bunk to Tamara and the boy.

"Are you sure?" she says.

Completely, I say.

"Thank you. I tried to get lower bunks for us, but they were all reserved."

I look at the young man in black, but he does not look at us.

I then ask Tamara if she would like us to leave, so that she and the boy can change.

"Could you? Thanks."

C'mon, I say to the young man. He retrieves a pack of Parliaments from a man purse of soft black leather, then walks to the space between cars.

I stand before a window in the corridor, look out. We are overtaking commuter trains on parallel rails, passing through districts whose names are spelled vertically, in neon, on the narrow sides of apartment buildings. Already we are nearing the outskirts of the city, the layout of which reflects the demographics of the country, at large: the farther from the center of power, the poorer the conditions for living.

Soon the street lights will be sparse, and I will be unable to see much. But if the route to Vurnary is like other routes out of Moscow, I know what I will be missing: factories that have lain dormant since the late eighties, or early nineties; apartment buildings of prefabricated concrete panels, the facades flaking, the balconies clogged with possessions; small electric substations, rusted, that deliver the lone public utility to villages whose residents, with their wells and outhouses, live much like Russians did before the October Revolution; toppled stools and crates on the sides of roads from which villagers sell milk and eggs and potatoes and apples and preserves to motorists; frames of metal poles over which people throw plastic tarps, and under which they sell cheap carpets, beach towels, stuffed animals, beaded car seats, and enormous bags of flour-and-sugar-based puffs.

The legendary expanses of the largest country on Earth are rarely visible from the windows of trains.

I hear the door of the compartment slide open. When I turn, Tamara is seated on my former bunk with Gena. She has not changed, but she has changed the boy. She is passing him wedges of pear from the blade of a knife.

The radio is broadcasting a different song, "You're a Woman," another hit from the eighties. It is by Bad Boys Blue, a German group that sings in English.

> Tonight. There'll be no darkness tonight.
> Hold tight. Let your love light shine bright.
> Listen to my heart—and lay your body next to mine.
> Let me fill your soul with all my dreams.

> You're a woman. I'm a man.
> This is more than just a game.
> I can make you feel so right.
> Be my lady of the night.

Tamara asks me where I am from, and where I am going. I tell her. I ask Tamara where she is from, where she is going. She tells me she grew up near Sochi, a resort area on the Black Sea. Now she is living in Moscow, where she is studying fashion design. She is separated from her husband, and delivering their son for a visit with her mother-in-law.

This will be her first New Year's alone, she says. She expects to feel lonely over the holiday—by far the country's biggest—because just about everything, everywhere, shuts down for a couple weeks.

> Lay Back. Back in my tenderness.
> And take. Take all of my sweet caress.
> You've got all of me—it can't go wrong if you agree.
> Soon two hearts will beat in ecstasy.

> You're a woman. I'm a man.
> This is more than just a game.
> I can make you feel so right.
> Be my lady of the night.

The conductor has not brought the tea. I get up to get it.

As I walk along the corridor I glance into other compartments—at the young women in stretch pants and loose T-shirts, the young men in slacks and wife-beater undershirts, the older men in sateen track suit bottoms, and the older women in sweaters. All have removed their shoes.

At the threshold of the control room I peek in. The conductor is sitting on the lower bunk, cross-checking the names on the tickets against the names in a ledger. A box of halvah and a glass of tea, a spoon upright in the glass, are on the pop-up table.

Hello, again, I say. Are you particularly busy right now?

"Sit, sit." She motions to the bunk with her head. She has taken off her cap. Her hair is dyed a dark red.

I sit next to her. She is holding a forefinger up to the draft from the thin space between the window and the window pane. She notices that I have noticed.

"I burned it on the hot water tank."

I am reminded of a story an acquaintance told me about summers in the Soviet Union, during which he worked off his college tuition as a conductor on a train that ran between Moscow and Krasnoyarsk, a large city in Siberia. He and a friend once hung a sheet of plastic in the corridor, in the space around the hot water tank. Then they splashed hot water onto the tank, producing steam.

A makeshift banya. On a train.

The conductor rolls up the last of the tickets, slips it into the notebook.

"How can I be of use to you?"

I ask her how long till we get to Vurnary. It is not on the list of scheduled stops.

"What are you going to do there?"

I am not obliged to tell her, but I do.

The conductor says it is hard to believe that a foreigner would be so interested in banya culture, let alone know anything about it. She refers to modern banyas as white banyas, which, indeed, is what they are called. But she is the only person I have met who calls them that. No one says he is going to steam white-style, or *po-belomu*. He just steams.

"No day without a line," she says.

It is a reference to my journalism. It also is a saying by Pliny the Elder that is better known in Russia as the title of a popular memoir by Yury Olesha, a Soviet novelist. Censors allowed the book to be published only posthumously, in 1961.

The conductor is not originally from Chuvashiya. She moved there—with her husband of twenty-eight years, and their two daughters—from Turkmenistan, a former Soviet republic (then known as Turkmeniya) on the Caspian Sea. Like most ethnic Russians from Central Asia, she left after the Soviet collapse. The decision to leave was made easier after she lost a job assembling appliances at a factory, then her father died. By the time she and her family moved, she was lining up, morning and night, for bread.

She wells up. "We had four seasons there. Ohh."

"We built two houses in a valley for them, for the kids. Oh, how beautiful it is here in the summer. The forest. Clean air."

It is as if she is talking about the newly dead: she says here, but means there.

She does not like her job, she says, but she is made for it.

"I saw them, the young mother and child. Upper bunks."

I already offered them my bunk, I say.

"Of course you did. You're not like ours."

Certainly she could not have known about the young patriot?

Once, she says, an elderly couple traveled in her car to the eye clinic of the late Svyatoslav Fyodorov, an ophthalmologist and microsurgeon who invented radial keratotomy, which involves cutting the pupil to correct vision. The couple shared a compartment with two thirty-something men, each of whom had a lower bunk. The conductor asked the men to give up their bunks, but they refused.

"What could I do? I couldn't force them."

She helped the elderly couple climb into their bunks on narrow, collapsible ladders. Then, later that night, the conductor was awakened by knocking on her door. It was the elderly woman, who reported that her head was spinning. The conductor gave the woman her bunk. Several minutes later the husband, nearly blind, groped his way along the corridor to check on his wife.

"I went back to the compartment and said, 'God forbid this happens to your parents! God forbid you get old like that!'"

The young men did not even look up from their newspapers.

"Vurnary, right? Not many get off there."

Will you still be awake by then? I ask. If so, would you be able to wake me up?

"Sure," she says. "We have a wake-up service."

I have traveled tens of thousands of miles on trains in Russia. This is the first time I have heard of a wake-up service.

"Fifty rubles."

Oh. If I pay her fifty rubles, or $2, she will wake me up.

Deal, I say.

I am emboldened. I propose buying a tea glass and the metal holder into which it nests, a *podstakannik*. (The word is generous in its logic: *pod* means under, and *stakannik* is the diminutive for drinking glass.) The design on the metal holder is of an oasis with palm trees—not Russian so much as a Russian dream.

I offer her 500 rubles, or $13, about half of which should cover the costs of replacement, and the remainder of which, say, could be donated to a favorite charity.

The conductor is quiet.

I plan on giving it to my mom, I say. And, truly, I do.

"Okay," she says. "Just in case, don't tell anyone where you got it."

Just about everything is for sale in Russia. And just about everyone, too.

When I get back to my compartment all are in bed. Tamara is in an upper bunk, a book against bent knees, feet beneath a blanket. She has washed her face, let down her hair.

I take off my boots, lock the door, and climb into my bunk. I lay down on my back, unbutton my jeans, push them to my knees. As I sit up to slide them off I feel fat, self-conscious. I am wearing a T-shirt, black, and boxers, yellow goldfish on a field of orange. Black, I have read, is slimming.

I pull the comforter over myself, retrieve a notepad and a pen. I turn down the volume of the radio, which is playing "American Boy," a song by Kombinaciya, a Russian girl group from the eighties.

I play the balalaika.
It is the most Russian instrument.
I dream of living in Jamaica.
In Jamaica, there are no balalaikas.

And there is no happiness in my personal life.
My years are passing by in vain.
So where are you my foreign prince?
Come for me faster. I am waiting for you.

American boy, American joy,
American boy for always time.
American boy, I am leaving with you.
I am leaving with you—Goodbye, Moscow.

I look over at Tamara. She is a student of fashion design in one of the world's fashion-obsessed cities. A balalaika, a triangular stringed instrument essential to Russian folk music, is likely as exotic to her as it would be to a foreigner watching a troupe of folk dancers, on tour, in a foreign city.

She is not a simple Russian girl. I feel as if she is three steps ahead of me, as if she almost can divine what I am thinking. She smiles to herself, as if she is thinking the same thing, too.

She turns to me, whispers, "So, are you going to teach me how to clean out a banya?"

She smiles, reaches for my yellow legal pad, and pen. She draws a picture of a small tub made of wood, the kind in which bathers might soak their bundles of leafy twigs. She writes the name, *kadyk*, underneath.

"You probably have a girl," she says. "Probably, you're popular with girls."

In matters of taste and color, I say.

It is a fragment from a saying that goes: In matters of taste and color, there are no comrades.

"Besides," she says, "pity always arouses sympathy in women."
Oh.

I ask if she means pity as in pity, or some nuance of the word.

"That's right, pity."

She places her forefingers directly beneath her eyes.

"A little bit sad."

She smiles. Big.

I do not smile big with Tamara. I cannot.

Perhaps she is right? Perhaps overthinking and self-intimidation have blunted my joy? Perhaps the personal slights and low-level aggression of daily life here, the ever-present need to display invulnerability, have made me a little bit sad?

I long have been aware that I smile less in Russia. But people here simply smile less; a smile that is too big, too ready, engenders distrust. Russian smiles, when they appear, tend to be sincere. I long have been aware, too, that I laugh less. Laughter here emanates more from my head, than my heart. I never, ever, laugh until my stomach hurts. Not ever.

At least I arouse feelings within Tamara, albeit feelings of pity. Certainly she is not indifferent. She has told me that she is single, that she will be childfree, and that she does not want to be alone over the holidays. I think this is when I am supposed to ask for her phone number.

But I do not ask. Even though I crave connection, physical and otherwise, I crave simplicity even more. Too many things in my life seem to be coming to an end for me to start anything new. Besides, what do I have to offer a single mother from Russia? I am the worst kind of American boy. Certainly I can be a lover, and a partner, but I do not want to be a parent, or a husband. I like nice things, but I long have lived without them. Moreover, I do not own a house, or an apartment, or a car. I do not even own a bicycle. By Moscow standards, I am a loser.

"Time for bed," she says.

She shuts off her light, pulls up her blanket, and turns her back to me.

Goodnight, I say.

I am tired, but I cannot sleep. I dig out from my rucksack a collection of stories by Anton Chekhov. The collection is hard to find outside of a library, and libraries in Russia do not lend books. I brought it because it contains a short story titled "In the Banya"—not that I really ever need a reason to read Chekhov.

The story revolves around a barber in a banya that resembles the country's most famous bathhouse, the Sandunovsky Baths in Moscow; Chekhov occasionally steamed there in the late 1800s. At that time barbers not only cut hair, but let blood through the placement of glass cups, or leeches. The story is like much of Chekhov—somehow engrossing, and meaningful, even though it does not have a climax or clear point at the end. I take particular note of one sentence: "Scholarship, in conjunction with poverty, bear evidence to the high qualities of the soul."

I resolve to transcribe it, and to stick it to the mirror in my foyer.

I shut off the reading light. Within minutes my vision of the banya in Chekhov is overtaken by the vision of the black banya in my mind. Always, it is the same.

I am making my way on foot, alone, through a forest of dense white birch and slim, singular pines. It is late summer, the cold snap that precedes Indian summer. Abruptly the forest ends, and I am looking down a slope of soft grasses toward a clearing where a banya stands, alone.

Its clapboard façade is bleached by the weather, and streaked black by corroding nails. It has a small window, closed, and a low door, ajar, from which smoke tumbles out, up and up.

There are no other people in my image. There is no sound. The banya is smoldering, seething, yet passive. My vision is kind of spooky, I realize, as if it were from a fairytale of the Brothers Grimm. Even the forest is keeping its distance.

For what is engulfed by smoke, but does not burn? Where else does water coexist with fire? What good can be found in a building that is enchanted by a goblin with bad intentions?

Perhaps, in a handful of hours, I will find out.

I am awakened by the tap-tap-tapping of a key against the door. I drop to the floor, open the door, thank the conductor. I dress in the dark, grab my boots, my coat, my bag, and step into the corridor. I slide closed the door.

I am saying goodbye to the conductor when I see Tamara walking down the corridor, smiling.

"So, are you going to teach me how to clean out a banya?"

I write down her phone numbers, say goodbye.

The train rolls smoothly to a stop. The conductor throws open the door of the car, and the air hits me like a snowball in the face. My eyes, with all the pity that they elicit, begin to water.

I look out. Moonlight reflects brightly off fresh snow that would be covering the platform, if there were one.

The conductor steps back, arms folded inside her coat. She does not put down the steps.

No platform? I say.

"Nope!"

No steps?

"Nope!"

You want me to jump?

"Yep! Just jump!" she says, smiling.

I pause. It is a six-foot drop into snow that might be concealing debris, or a ditch. I recall a story from fifth grade about an older boy in town who leapt from the railroad trestle into the creek. A railroad spike pierced the space between his asshole and his balls.

"Seriously, be quick about it. The train is about to start rolling again!"

The train inches forward, jars to a stop. The engineer is pulling taut the cars.

I jump. The extra weight from my bag pushes me deeper into the snow, which reaches my hips. My mouth falls open as dry cold jabs up my back, and inside the cuffs of my jeans.

I turn my head, look up, laugh. The conductor laughs, too.

"Hurry! Run!" She scans the parallel rails for a lone white headlight.

The train begins to roll. She waves, twice, then shuts the door with a thwack.

I stand still in the snow. Snowflakes are not so much falling as floating in the air like a fine glass powder. Electricity pings along the wires overhead.

I move through the snow with knees high, as if bashing through breakers in an ocean. Outside the train station I beat ice crystals from my jeans, stomp them from the laces of my boots. Two men are standing next to cars that are idling, headlights on. I do not see Maria and Gennady. I do not see them inside the train station, either. In fact, I do not see anyone, even though two duffel bags are on a bench, and another bag is on the floor.

This is unusual. Not even the homeless leave bags unattended in Russia.

The station is a high-ceilinged hall with walls of pink and white. There is no heat emanating from the radiators, large pipes welded into the shape of tuning forks. There is no cell phone coverage. There is no clock.

I am too cold to sit, so I stand and wait.

I hear the station doors close. An elderly woman shuffles in. She is wearing orange mittens and three headscarves, brown wool over white wool over a colorful print.

Hello, I say.

She does not acknowledge me.

I hear the doors close, again. Two men walk in. They have come to meet someone who has not arrived. They look Russian, but they are not speaking Russian. They are speaking a language I have never heard, one that does not resemble any language I have ever heard. They leave.

"Unclear if they'll be meeting you," the elderly woman says to me. "Better take a cab. It's cold out."

She did not ignore me. She is simply hard of hearing.

I do not want to haggle over a fare when I do not know where I am going. I also do not want to display a lack of faith in Maria and Gennady, to whom I am grateful.

More minutes pass. The ticket window opens. I approach the woman behind the glass.

Good morning, I say loudly into the glass.

She looks at me, looks away.

Do you have any maps for sale?

She shakes her head.

You don't by any chance happen to know where Ashmarova Street is, do you?

No response.

"Come with me. I'll show you," the elderly woman says.

She begins to walk, so I follow. Apparently the unattended bags are not hers.

The woman is wearing Russian boots of black wool felt with rubber soles. I am wearing American boots of waterproof leather. I take particular note because, on the streets, I am struggling to keep pace; my longtime brand was retooled for hip-hop hipsters while I was out of the country, and the soles now become slippery in the cold.

I shuffle, slide, shuffle, slide through snowflakes that have settled like ash, white and weightless, over the ice. The light from scarce streetlights reflects off glass in windows and sharp angles of buildings, but is lost in the shadow of inscrutable detail.

I feel as if we are moving through the frames of a black-and-white comic strip.

"Already I'm seventy-three, dying," the woman says.

If she had told me she was ninety-two, I would have believed her.

She is taking shallow, audible breaths. Her nose is running, and her eyes are tearing. She says a doctor recently gave her a shot, but it only made her feel worse.

Were the men speaking Chuvash in the train station? I ask.

"I can't read. I'm not a scientist. Almost blind already. All my life—goats, chickens. Now, I'm lazy."

She lapses into what I assume is Chuvash, then says, in Russian, "You're not from here."

I tell her that I am from Moscow. I do not offer that I am American.

"Guys go there for work, don't come back."

I say that I have come to meet friends of a friend, and to steam in a black banya. We do not have authentic black banyas in Moscow, I say. There, it costs 600 rubles to steam for two hours.

"*Ukh*, they only know how to print money there! By the time you undress, dress, two hours? Can that really be called a banya?"

I do not say anything.

"Here, twenty rubles, wash as long as you want."

We pass what appears to be the town hall, in the courtyard of which a tall pine is strung with multicolored bulbs. A banner says something in Chuvash.

The woman says she remembers when young people went to dances for New Year's. "Back in the old days," she says, "the money was smaller, but we lived better."

The street dead ends at another street. She stops. I stop.

She points one way, waves her hand as if shooing a fly, then walks the other way.

Goodbye, I say. A huge thank you.

She does not look back.

It is exhilarating to be walking alone, in the dark of morning, in an unknown direction, in an unfamiliar town. I am warm except for my cheekbones and upper molars, the space where bone meets bone. Ahead, beyond an intersection, I see a young boy standing in the middle of the street. His arms are at his sides, and he is wearing a dark skullcap. He is looking toward me.

When I reach him I say hello, ask if he knows the house I am looking for.

The boy says nothing, but turns and walks to a two-story wooden house. I follow him. He opens a door, walks up a flight of stairs, and opens another door, to an apartment. I follow him inside, into a warmth that smells of breakfast. Light from multicolored bulbs glints off garland strung over the branches of a fir tree, fresh.

A petite woman in a red sweater comes into the room, apologizes, says that she and her husband overslept because they had been up most of the night partying with friends who had come over to try out the new karaoke machine beneath the tree. It is Maria.

Maria is naturally pretty, with pale skin and short dark hair. She implores me to call her Masha, introduces me to her sons, Dima, the boy from the street, and Sergei, a teenager. Gennady comes into the room, introduces himself, says I can call him Gena. He looks a bit like Viktor Tsoi, or how the Soviet-era rocker might have looked if he had lived into his thirties.

In the kitchen Masha, Gena, and I drink tea and talk. I give them a half dozen bags of premium coffee beans from around the world.

We do not linger.

Masha makes a phone call. Within minutes we are on the street and climbing into a white Zhiguli Model Four, a small passenger car. Like most Russian cars, the clearance between the chassis and the ground is high to account for the poor condition of the roads. That is fortunate, because the road out of town is not plowed. It is one lane, really. Or, rather, it is two icy ruts.

The car carries us swiftly over the dips and rises of farmland nearly bereft of trees. I do not ask where we are going. The trunks of trees spared the axe are whipped white by snow blown across the fields.

The crowns of the trees are brown, bare.

The horizon is indistinct, white fields against white sky.

I feel small in the backseat as we move through this expanse, this flaunting of open space. I recall passages from Dmitry Likhachev, the noted academic:

> Open space has always been dear to the hearts of Russians. It spills over into concepts and ideas which do not exist in other languages. How, for example, does freedom differ from liberty? It differs in that freedom is unrestricted, it is liberty combined with expanse, with anything not circumscribed by space. . . . Freedom is the vast space through which a person can walk and walk, wander, swim with the current of wide rivers and for great distances, and breathe the free air, the air of the wide open spaces.
>
> For a long time Russian culture has considered freedom and expanse the greatest aesthetic and ethical blessing of mankind. . . . Now look at the map of the world: the Russian plain is the largest on Earth. Did the plain determine Russian character, or did the Eastern Slavic tribes settle on the plain because it suited their spirit?

The Chuvash are not Slavs. They are descendants of Volga Bulgars who mixed with Finno-Ugric tribes some 1,500 years ago. Their language is the lone survivor of a distinct branch of Turkic languages that cannot be understood by speakers of other Turkic tongues.

Both Masha and Gena are ethnic Chuvash, but only Gena looks non-Russian. Each speaks Russian and Chuvash, but neither has spoken since we got into the car: the echo of the engine off the berm of snow, as high as the chassis, obliviates other sound.

Gena leans into me, "You don't know how lucky I am." He smiles, nods toward Masha in the front passenger's seat.

They have been together some twenty years. In fact, they both work at the same printing plant. He works as a guard, and she helps put out the twice-weekly newspaper, *The Path to Victory*, or *Put' Pobedy*. He earns 1,200 rubles per month, and she earns 1,800. Their salaries are take-home figures from which 1,360 rubles must be set aside for heat, water, and electricity—and 390 rubles, or a flat 13 percent, must be set aside for taxes.

Their combined monthly income, after expenses, is not enough to steam for even five hours at my chosen bathhouse in Moscow.

The biggest employers in Vurnary are a meat plant and a chemical plant. But the best jobs are with the railroad, which pays some 10,000 rubles per month. Gena sometimes travels for weeks at a time to Moscow, where he works as a laborer to help make ends meet.

The car moves fast, perhaps too fast, over the icy ruts. A bottle of Volzhanka mineral water rolls spasmodically over the rear dash each time the tires career within the ruts; like the grooves on the tracks of slot-car racers, the ruts are the only things keeping the Model Four from running off the road.

I cast a look of mild concern at Gena.

He smiles, leans forward, begins to shout out a joke.

An American, a German, and a Russian are riding in a car. The American boasts that American roads are so fine, so level, that one could place a glass of water on the hood of a car and the liquid would not spill. The German says that German roads are so fine, so level, that the water would not even jiggle in the glass. The Russian says that he, too, could place a glass of water on the hood of a car, but why bother? The ruts in the roads are so deep that all he has to do is step on the gas, and the car steers itself—leaving him free to bang a woman in the driver's seat.

Our driver lifts his hands from the wheel. He does not decelerate. He is showing me that there is more truth, than humor, in the joke.

Minutes later we come upon a village. The driver slows, stops at an intersection of two dirt roads, apparently the only roads in Malye Yaushi. He shuts off the engine. Masha makes a phone call. Moments later a man walks out of a house down a street, waves an arm in a slow arc. It is Vyacheslav. The house is not his, but the black banya is.

We greet each other, shake hands. Vyacheslav tells me to call him Slava. Then we line up shoulder to shoulder for a photo: Gena, me, Slava, then two boys named Kolya. Irretrievably American, I smile. I am the only one who does.

Slava slides open a heavy wooden gate and we walk into the yard. A puppy, part German Shepherd, comes out from a hole in a wall of a barn. It cowers and rolls onto its back, shivering. A thermometer shows minus 7 degrees Fahrenheit.

Masha turns to go inside the house, a one-story wooden cottage. We, the men, do not. We turn toward the black banya. "It's better to see it once than to hear about it a hundred times," Gena says.

The banya resembles a rustic cabin with a peaked roof and two small rooms. The door is ajar, and Gena and I follow Slava into a narrow foyer with coat hooks and a bench. Two low doors are on either side of us. One leads to the washroom. The other leads to the steam room. Slava opens the door to the steam room and we duck beneath the transom, inside.

In a corner opposite the door sits an open-faced brick stove. On top of the stove sits a mound of rocks the size of potatoes. The rocks are encrusted with a powdery soot. Inches above the rocks hangs a cast iron cauldron from a hook in the ceiling. Both the cauldron and the ceiling are black from soot, a black that is glossier than that on the rocks. The dark sheen spreads from the ceiling, like dusk, over the upper reaches of the walls.

On a shelf the upper half of a box of laundry detergent is black, and the lower half is a swirl of white, yellow, and orange.

Next to the stove are two benches, one higher than the other. Each is wide enough for a person to lie upon. Opposite the stove is a window, beneath which stretches a long, low bench.

"The banya is fairly new," Slava says, "but it was built according to old technology."

Slava stands too straight and the top of his muskrat hat smudges black against the ceiling. He squats and rights the crooked hat, the flaps of which flare hang-dog-like over his ears.

He says he normally would have begun to heat the banya hours ago, but he chose to wait in order to show me how he does it. Heating a stove is never perfunctory.

Slava takes me outside to a shed that is stacked high with birch, cured and quartered. A fresh sheep skin hangs from a rafter. He lays lengths of birch into the crooks of my arms, then places a piece of pine on top. Inside the steam room he shaves off strips of the pine

On the sill of the window opposite the bench are reminders of the continued utility of the banya: it is not only a place to steam, but to wash. A toothbrush. Slivers of soap. A small glass.

with a knife, piles the shavings inside the stove, and lights them on fire. He stacks the birch around the mound of flame.

We squat on our haunches, quiet, and watch the flames spread. I recall the short story by the Soviet author, Vasily Shukshin, about a single-minded collective farmer whose passion is heating his banya on Saturdays, the traditional banya day. The farmer's name is Kostya Valikov, but his comrades call him Alyosha Beskonvoinyi because of his "rare in our days irresponsibility, uncontrollability."

Beskonvoinyi literally means without escort. A prisoner who is trusted more than other prisoners sometimes may go about his day *beskonvoinyi*, or without escort.

"On Saturday he stoked the banya. That's all. Nothing else," writes Shukshin. "He made the banya red hot, washed, and began to steam. He steamed like he was deranged, like a steam engine—he steamed for five hours! With stops to rest, of course, with smoking breaks. . . . But, even still—you need some kind of constitution! Maybe a horse's?"

Like Slava, Alyosha Without Escort heats his stove with birch. He believes birch is imbued with spirit that can be felt, or sensed, in the heat. Birch burns long, even. Birch does not burn hot. The heat from birch is a steady heat.

Like us, Alyosha Without Escort also likes to sit on his haunches and watch the flames. Only, whereas I am thinking about him, in the story he is thinking to himself: "So you there want that all people lived the same way . . . Two logs burn differently, and you want all people to live the same way!"

Once his fire is stoked Alyosha Without Escort relaxes, drinks tea. By the time the logs are ruby embers, Shukshin writes, the stove is so hot that the steam it generates clings to his ears and climbs into his throat, even into his psyche. "All sorts of harmful tension completely let go of Alyosha, petty thoughts abandoned his head, a kind of wholeness, significance, clarity settled into his soul—life made sense. That is to say life was near, beyond the small window of the bathhouse, but Alyosha was inaccessible to her, to her fuss and spite. He became big and indulgent."

Slava and I watch the pine shavings turn to ash, their flame subsumed by the birch. I am aware that I, too, am feeling somehow big, indulgent. Certainly I am feeling grateful. To Nataliya. And to Masha. And to Gena. And to Slava. And to Chekhov, and Shukshin, all those who wrote what they knew so that I, too, could know.

I look up. Smoke is agitating slow and thick at the ceiling. I am reminded of how it feels to look up at the sky while underwater, just below the surface of the ocean.

It occurs to me that a flue, a chimney, has been the greatest innovation in the history of the banya.

Slava stands, grabs two battered pails. Gena and I follow him outside and across the yard, a long, rectangular plot bordered by a fence and a line of birch. A boy, one of the Kolyas, joins us.

Scattered across the property are rounded haystacks, snowbound. On a clothesline hang shirts and pants, frozen stiff. Inside the barn a cow is pregnant with what Slava is certain is another bull; soon he

Gena carries birch logs, cured and quartered, into the steam room to heat the stove. Birch burns long, and steady, and is imbued with spirit that can be felt, or sensed, in the heat, Slava says.

either will slaughter the cow, or pay someone to take it, because no one wants a cow that births only bulls.

"Life is lived poorly in Chuvashiya," Slava says.

"The Chuvash are a poor people," adds Gena.

Slava sets down the pails on an apron of iced-over snow at the base of a large wooden box with a lid. The box, too, is slathered in ice, flash-frozen splashes that resemble a waterfall in stop action.

Kolya lifts the lid. With bare hands he pulls up some sixteen feet of chain, at the end of which is a bucket heavy with water. He dumps the water into the pails. By the time we carry the pails back to the steam room a thin skin of ice has stretched over the water's surface. Smoke already is slinking past the door, into the bright gray sky.

In some regions the black banya is known as the smoke banya, or *kurnaya* banya.

We crouch low as Slava pours some of the water into the cauldron.

Slava scoops hot water from a cauldron in the young coals of the open-flame stove in the steam room, which is still being heated. He ladles the water into the shallow metal basin on the floor, to his right, in which he will soak a bundle of leafy birch twigs.

He leaves the rest in the pails, which he places on the highest bench. Although the smoke is visible above us, seemingly separate, the carbon monoxide gas, I suspect, is not. As if on cue Masha appears in the doorway, tells us to get out before we are poisoned.

Slava stabs more wood into the stove. We leave.

Outside Gena lights a cigarette. He recounts that, as a boy, on a Chuvash holiday that is similar in spirit to Thanksgiving, he lost consciousness in a black banya because he inhaled too much of the gas. He was carried outside, where he revived in the fresh air.

"Literally on the day of thanks I was made to sustain that very thing. My parents were very happy their child remained alive."

Carbon monoxide poisoning is a risk that is inherent to black banyas. It is one of the reasons they are unpopular. Another is that they require more work: the steam room should be aired out, and the walls and ceiling swabbed with a wet rag, before steaming. Still,

The younger Kolya stands beneath the smoke churning out the doorway of the steam room as the stove is heated. The smoke leaves a sheen of soot on the boards above the transom of the door—the signature of the black banya. Carbon monoxide in the smoke always presents a danger.

the greatest danger in a black banya—in all banyas—is fire. Hundreds of Russians die each year in fires that originated in banyas. Usually the fires are sparked by electrical malfunctions resulting from shoddy construction. Sometimes, though, the culprit is drunkenness.

People make mistakes when they are drunk.

Sometimes they simply pass out.

Gena stubs out his cigarette in the hard snow, glances at the banya. Smoke also has begun to rise in wisps from gaps at the peak of the roof. We turn, walk toward the house.

In the foyer we take off our boots and put on communal slippers or stockings of a pliant wool felt. Long-faded photographs and magazine clippings hang in frames angled at the junctures of the walls with the ceiling. One clipping commemorates the 1962 spaceflight of Vostok 3, which was piloted by the cosmonaut Andriyan Nikolaev, an ethnic Chuvash who later married the first woman in space, Valentina Tereshkova.

We pass through a door into a large room that truly could be called a living room since nearly all aspects of domestic life transpire within. The room is dominated by a Russian oven, white, which divides the room into a small kitchen, a small bedroom, and a large sitting room with a divan, a table, and a television. The table is smothered with food, and bounded by people, about a dozen.

"We don't speak English," someone says in Russian, "but we promise not to laugh when you speak Russian."

I smile, laugh—threaten not to speak Russian.

I am unprepared for such a reception. I am wearing jeans, whereas an elderly woman is dressed in an ethnic Chuvash wedding dress, hers, and an elderly man is wearing a suit and tie. I have come with empty hands, whereas the women must have been cooking for at least two days, and preparing for even longer.

The owner of the house introduces herself as Tyotya Zoya, or Aunt Zoya. She is in her early sixties, about the same age as my mom. She is wearing a headscarf and an apron. Someone rises from his seat at the table, and Aunt Zoya tells me to take it.

Before me are small pies, some filled with pork, others with cabbage. There are sprats in oil, from the Baltic Sea, and imitation crab sticks. There are salads—fresh beets in a vinaigrette, and fresh coleslaw. There are marinated white mushrooms, Slippery Jack mushrooms, and some other kind of mushroom. There are pickles, homemade, and a plum jelly, also homemade. There are boiled potatoes, and pig's blood fried with garlic. There is a bottle of a local vodka infused with honey. There is a bottle of a clear moonshine infused with plums, and another flavored by a small, fresh cucumber. There is a teakettle, too, that is not filled with tea, but unfiltered beer that was made by Aunt Zoya from hops that she grew and gathered herself.

Aunt Zoya calls in her daughter from the kitchen. Irina, who is married to Slava, does not drink. But today she is making an exception. In fact, she makes the first toast, to acquaintanceship.

I am in a mood to keep drinking, and to begin eating, but I resolve to hold back until we have steamed. My resolve is tested by Aunt Zoya, who fills my glass with beer from the kettle, then opens a bottle of moonshine, laughs, and says, "Folk medicine heals you. Here, have some folk medicine."

She makes the next toast, "So that the steam will be hot!"

I notice a religious icon—nearly obscured by a handmade doily—on a high shelf in the corner opposite the Russian oven, in keeping with Russian Orthodox tradition. I also notice, on the floor of the bedroom, a nearly lifeless black-and-white goat kid; Slava castrated it the previous day so that its meat would taste sweeter.

I apologize to Aunt Zoya, to everyone, say that I had not known that we would be coming here, to Malye Yaushi, otherwise I would not have arrived with empty hands.

I am told not to worry, that my reporting is something they respect, but cannot do, in turn. I am told it is more meaningful, even, than what they are doing for me.

I ask, too, that no one takes offense at my seemingly small appetite. I will eat and drink after we have steamed, I say.

"Eat and drink as much as you want," Aunt Zoya says. "You can, you can, you always can, if you're careful."

Besides, she says, we will not be eating the food in front of us— at least not until we all share a soup of thin gray broth made from the heart, lungs, liver, feet, and tail of a pig. "The Chuvash are a

Aunt Zoya—her back to the massive, whitewashed Russian oven—makes a toast: "So that the steam will be hot!" She brewed the beer with hops she grows herself.

poor people," Aunt Zoya says. "We use every part of the animal."

The soup, *shurbe*, is the first course at Chuvash weddings. Guests lose their appetites for everything else because they eat so much *shurbe*, Aunt Zoya tells me.

I picture a bride with gray dribbles down the front of her gown.

"No one likes it the first time."

Aunt Zoya brings out a burlap sack, shows me the hops from which she made the beer. They flake in her cupped hands—the wings of insects. She motions me to the root cellar beneath the kitchen floor, shows me the carrots, beets, squash, preserves, and potatoes. Some potatoes are for eating, and others are for planting.

Back in the living room the elderly woman in the wedding dress, Zina, a neighbor, sings a folk song in Chuvash.

I stand, propose a toast, the third toast. I toast to the owner of the home, to Aunt Zoya, who begins to weep. She says something in

Chuvash and gestures toward the icon, hands high.

She asks me to pass along her best wishes to my mother. "Friends may meet, but mountains never greet," she says.

I am beginning to feel buzzed. I have had three shots of vodka, and one of moonshine, plus several small glasses of beer. My thoughts begin to pull me out of the moment.

It only makes sense that I have come here, to Chuvashiya, to the site of a black banya, the mystical dimension of a banya culture, during a period of transition: banya lore holds that forces of change are more powerful during transitions.

Slava leaves to check on the temperature of the steam room. When he returns he smiles, says, "Let's go."

I retrieve my banya hat from my rucksack, but not my flip-flops: I want to feel the wood, its grain, on the soles of my feet.

Slava already is in the steam room by the time Gena and I get there. We strip down. I begin to hang my clothes on hooks, then stop, drop everything into a pile; the foyer is unheated, and temperatures have fallen. I open the door to the steam room and duck below the transom, pass through. The steam room is not as hot as I expected, especially at the floor, where the cold from the ground can be felt through spaces between planks. It would not be this way if it were not for me, if Slava had heated the banya as long as usual.

Slava scoops hot water from the cauldron and ladles it over the rocks. The room fills fast with a steam that chastens the chill. The steam is soft, enveloping. It also is sharp, and carries a mildly sulfurous scent.

I recall the sensation of a metal fork coming too close to the crown over one of my molars.

The three of us sit silently on the benches, experience the steam. We smile. Stray threads of soot hang in the air. Some settle in splotches onto the white felt of my hat.

We did not swab the walls with water.

Slava stands up, pours hot water from a pail into a metal basin that holds a bundle of leafy birch twigs. Immediately the room is overcome by the scent of the leaves. The scent is so powerful that I feel we are smelling the essence of the entire tree from which they

Aunt Zoya, coatless in subzero temperatures, holds a cauldron containing the freshly slaughtered makings of *shurbe*, a national dish of the Chuvash people.

Poised to drink down the first toast in the living room of Aunt Zoya's home. From left to right: Aunt Zoya, the author, Gena, Zina, Irina, and Masha. More food, and drinks, are to come.

came, for I have never smelled leaves with a scent this rich—and I have steamed in dozens of bathhouses, in the aroma of thousands of bundles of leafy twigs, over the past decade.

I attribute the power of the scent to the land, at first, to the pristine ecology. Then I realize the pungency has more to do with the banya: the smoke, the soot on the ceiling and upper walls, serves as an antiseptic that, like a needle disinfected by flame, kills off lingering microbes. The scent of the birch is so rich because it is so pure.

It is the best smell I have ever encountered in a banya.

Slava dilutes beer from the kettle with water. He ladles the mixture onto the rocks, and the scent of hops overwhelms the scent of birch. The mixture is a bit too heavy with beer, though; briefly the steam stings my eyes.

Gena says okay, he is going to do it, he is going to beat me with the fragrant birch twigs.

"Are you ready?" he says.

I lie down on my stomach upon the highest bench, my feet toward the stove. Slava throws more water onto the rocks and my legs fold instinctively at the knees, move as far as possible from the hot burst of steam. As the steam begins to settle I allow my legs to fall. Gena begins to massage my shoulders and back with the birch leaves. Warmth moves deeper into my body with each successive blow of the birch, and I cannot help but feel that I am absorbing, too, the energy of the earth that fed the roots of the tree. The warmth spreads throughout my body like blood into an appendage that was stuck in one position for too long, and then was freed.

Gena's breathing is labored. "You're tough," he says.

Steam rises from the basin in which birch *veniki* are soaking in hot water. To the right, on the bench upon which bathers sit, or lie, a pail holds yet more hot water. To the left small stones covered in a powdery soot are mounded on top of the stove. A glossy sheen of soot covers the log walls.

He returns the birch twigs to the basin and ducks outside to join Slava, to cool.

I lie still for a moment. Then I push myself up, drop my legs over the bench, onto the floor. I sit quietly for a moment, two, before ducking through the door, to the other side. I do not need to brace myself against the cold.

Epilogue

Three times I have felt sure I was supposed to leave Russia in the same way I felt sure, in the nineties, that I was supposed to leave the States. Two of those times I ignored my intuition—by which I mean the information we always get, but only sometimes hear—because I wanted more of an inkling of what awaited me. It is risky to deny a calling, though, and, this time, the third time, I worry that the fates might conspire to take away my choices. So I am leaving.

Besides, I am getting a push.

Over the past several months agents of the FSB have taken an even more acute interest in my work, and life. I have not minded much that, for years, they have read my e-mails (a matter of public record), and listened in on my phone conversations (also a matter of public record). I have not even minded much that, over the past two years, they have intentionally introduced mistakes to documents I need to renew my visa and accreditation as a journalist. The other day, though, even the FSB told me it was time to go.

It was morning on a Saturday when I dropped by the Press Center of the Ministry of Foreign Affairs, in Moscow, to pick up a new sheaf of documents to extend my stay by another year. My so-called curator (accredited foreign journalists are assigned curators, or handlers) was waiting for me with a man he introduced as his boss. They invited me into a small room with a table and three chairs—two on one side, one on the other. Each motioned with a hand, and I sat. Then my curator placed a new accreditation card on the table between us as if to say that, no matter what happens in this room, nothing would change. But everything already had.

They grilled me about nearly all facets of my life not only in Russia, but before, in the States. They were especially interested to learn about my ethnic heritage (did I have Jewish blood in my family?), and my volunteer work with the homeless in Moscow. In fact, they asked me about nearly everything except the reason they had ambushed me in the first place: I was slated the next day to fly to Nalchik, the capital of the southwestern Kabardino-Balkaria Republic, to interview, on behalf of a colleague, the father of Aleksander Litvinenko—the Russian spy who was fatally poisoned in London in 2007 with a rare radioactive isotope, polonium-210, that had been slipped into his tea.

I do not care much for the story. The killing is audacious, to be sure, and a shock to Westerners, but there is no surprise in Russia when a former agent of the FSB is taken out by the organization he betrayed—an organization to which its members are more loyal than, even, their own country. Moreover, Litvinenko had taken up with a widely hated oligarch, Boris Berezovsky,* who has been trying to destabilize the Kremlin from exile.

Of course they took Litvinenko out.

I told the colleague I would help him report part of his book because it offered me a change of pace, and a little cash. It also was a challenge: I thought I could learn things other journalists could not.

Over ninety-some minutes, my interrogators attempted to outline in black the contours of a life Russian friends tend to characterize as that of a "free painter," or *svobodnyi khudozhnik*. I answered the questions candidly because, while I do not advertise the details of my life, I cannot be bothered to hide them.

I thought to say, but did not: "If you, or others, don't want me here, that is accomplished easily enough. *Mne takoi napryag ne nuzhen*," or "I don't need the hassle."

They were particularly interested, too, in the taxes I paid. And when the Ministry of Foreign Affairs inquires about taxes, it is not simply doing a favor for the State Tax Inspectorate.

Until that day I had deflected the added attention of curators through gifts of expensive whiskey around New Year's, and by hosting occasional bouts of late-night drinking at bars and nightclubs in the city. But the FSB is reinvigorated under Putin, and the disposition of curators toward foreign journalists is markedly . . . colder.

We did not shake hands after the interrogation ended, and I only

---

* Berezovsky died of a suspected suicide in London in early 2013.

noticed the mistake on my new accreditation card after I returned to my apartment. When I phoned the London-based reporter and told him what had happened, he called the episode a "shot across our bow" and asked me not to travel to interview the father.

"These guys play rough," he said.

I thought things had a ways to go, yet, before they got outright rough. The questions seemed to be meant primarily to intimidate me. At worst, I thought, I would have been detained in Nalchik—likely before I even had a chance to conduct the interview. It was possible I would have been roughed up, too, but I knew enough journalists that such an incident would be reported, which did not serve the interests of the FSB. I was more concerned about being falsely accused of a crime by some mid-level FSB officer looking "to make his epaulettes," as the expression goes in Russian—something I chronicled regularly while reporting on the persecution of Russian scientists. And even more than that I was concerned about being expelled from the country before I finished my research on banyas at the Russian State Library, the former Lenin Library, or *Leninka*, which overlooks the crenelated walls and golden domes of the Kremlin in which the former head of the FSB, Putin, holds sway.

Some two dozen books I had requested were still sitting on a shelf behind the desk of the reference librarians in Reading Hall No. 1, an exclusive reading room typically reserved—as stated clearly on the brass plate that hangs from its tall, wooden doors—"For Professors, Academicians, and Doctors of Science."

I am none of those. But, as a foreign correspondent since the mid-nineties, I was placed in the reading room at a time when the government still honored Soviet traditions of granting certain privileges to certain foreigners. Today the government is no longer enamored of foreigners, especially foreign journalists. Today I would be put in one of the reading rooms overcrowded with students.

But I am a holdover from another time. And I am grateful. For Reading Hall No. 1, like the banya, is a retreat from the grim energy of this megalopolis, and also from the things I do to avoid writing—sleeping, snacking, surfing the Internet, talking to friends, and chatting up women.

In the first hall the rules are different. I can request as many books as I want. I can keep them for two months, not two weeks. I can use a laptop irrespective of battery life; it is the only hall with electrical outlets. And I can labor at a solitary task among people, but not too many people—typically much older men in threadbare suits and down-at-the-heel shoes.

In Reading Hall No. 1 I can work at highly shellacked wooden tables, in the muted light of brass lamps with green lampshades, all but ensconced by exotic plants. Recently I counted seventy-six plants on the parquet floor, on the recessed window sills, and on the tops of the bookshelves that serve as privacy screens on the reading tables.

There are split-leaf philodendrons, and creeping vines native to tropical rainforests in Central America. There are spider plants and tubular white arum lilies native to Africa. There are jade plants and Christmas cacti. There are ferns and ivies. There are hoyas in bloom, and begonias and hibiscuses that are not. All were brought from home, by the librarians.

There is an orange tree. There are lemon trees, and young date palms with spindly leaves. All of them were grown from seeds of fruit eaten by the librarians, and their families, at home.

None of the trees actually bears fruit; this is the 55th parallel, after all. But the leaves of the plants are lush and, like all the surfaces in the reading hall, without dust.

Some of the plants—the palm tree from the Crimea, the coffee plant from Sochi, both on the Black Sea—were donated by readers.

When I moved to Russia I did not expect to see tropical plants. I expected gray skies, scarce sunlight, and long, cold, dark winters. Snow and vodka, yes. Split-leaf philodendrons, no. Yet just about everywhere I have reported in the country's eleven time zones—most memorably in dilapidated universities and scientific institutes—I have encountered similar tactile expressions of human spirit.

Less than three months remain until my visa expires. I tell the reporter in London that I can no longer help. Then I drop everything and dedicate six days a week—the library is closed on Mondays for cleaning—to finishing my research.

I decide not to renew my visa, and to mail to my mom's house stray possessions I do not give away. Then I will buy a last-minute ticket out of the country on a train to Finland. I decide, too, to say nothing of this to my curator.

I finish my research with more than a week to spare, by which time I have become accustomed to hearing a man's taxed breathing in the background of my cell phone conversations, and, sometimes, a woman's high heels along a corridor. I hear them so often, in fact, I suspect they are prerecorded.

In the intervening days I donate to the librarians in Reading Hall No. 1 the more than a dozen plants I have nurtured in the seven apartments I have rented in the city—plants native primarily to southern Africa, including two palm trees, one of which was grown from a coconut carried back from Sri Lanka.

I tell the librarians that, when this book is published, I will mail a copy to them. The librarians, all women, tell me that they will place the book in bookcase 43 N. 1, beneath the sign that says "Gifts from Readers." *With Light Steam* will sit on a shelf near Soviet-era books like *The Arithmetic of Infinity* and *Cosmonautics and Rocket Building,* and more recent titles like *From Where, and Toward What, Goes Russia?*

When I leave the country by train, less than two days before my visa expires, I am traveling heavier than usual. In addition to my lone travel backpack I am carrying seven liters of a not-for-export vodka, Veda, for a friend's wedding in Helsinki—well above the one-and-a-half-liter limit set by customs. I am leaving not only with mixed emotions, but mixed messages: I was told in the small room at the Foreign Affairs Ministry that I was no longer welcome, but I was told something else at the coat check on my last day at the library.

As an elderly woman in a blue smock laid my woolen overcoat on the counter, I asked her what would happen after I leave, after my library card expires. If I come back, I asked her, would I still be allowed to work in Reading Hall No. 1?

"Of course! Why wouldn't you?" she told me. "Just stand here, and you'll always get a special place. Just come right here, and we'll take care of you."

Appendix 1

Three Vignettes

Lyudmila's Bathing Ritual

The banya is like love at first sight, says Lyudmila Nikonova, an ethnographer from the Russian republic of Mordovia: "The first sensations are sometimes mistaken."

So Lyudmila plans days ahead to steam. If she is going to the banya, say, on a Saturday, she will dry coffee grounds on a kitchen plate for use in a body scrub. She will set aside a somewhat coarse salt, too, for use in a facial mask. She will do the housecleaning on Thursday, or Friday; no one wants to return from the banya to a mess, or spend the day after the banya cleaning.

"I like when things happen gradually," she says. "Some see each other, fall in love. That's it, love . . . Maybe that happens, that kind of thing. But I try to quash extremes in my life . . . so there isn't a powerful jolt later. It's the same with anything you do in the banya. There's no need for extremes. Do everything gradually.

"I very much like that Russian word, *mera*—proportion."

She will go to bed early the night before the banya because "a person should be rested" while steaming, and she likes to begin by eight o'clock in the morning, when there are few bathers.

"I don't like a crowd in the banya. When there's a crowd you need to talk, you need to support some kind of conversation. People carry with them some kind of news, they tell you all about what happened during the past week, and you're not wooden, you react to those events—you live out that information. And all of that—processing someone else's joy or grief through your body—is an added weight."

"Yet on Saturday and Sunday, I think, a person should take a break from her surroundings. It seems to me that, in the banya, you've got to forget about everything entirely. A person goes to the banya to relax," she says. "I've been steaming for about ten years with the same people, and we still don't know each other's names. No one asks how the other person is. We simply are quiet."

"We are united by one word—banya."

Once inside the bathhouse she undresses, makes her way to the steam room. "I simply sit there in the steam room, sort of come to myself. The first time in the steam room I walk around a bit, maybe swish the *venik* [through the air] . . . I feel alone with myself, alone."

After the first steam she will lightly scrub her skin with the salt to remove "build-up" from the past week. Then she will return to the steam room, where she will continue to lightly scrub her skin with a bath mitt. After the second steam she will rub the coffee grounds over her face and body, both exfoliating and softening the skin, before rinsing off and, sometimes, smearing her skin with honey— which is absorbed by her body in the steam room.

Sometimes she will use several types of *veniki* during the same steam—not only the popular birch, or oak. "I especially like fir *veniki* because when you steam with fir *veniki* the needles [lightly] prick your skin. In the summer I like very much to steam with *veniki* made from stinging nettles" that have been softened in water.

"Whenever I use a fir *venik*," which possesses an aromatic oil, "I always sleep well."

After the third or fourth steam she will wash up—usually while seated, feet soaking in a basin of warm water—with soap to which she adds some of the salt. Then she will wash her hair, and rinse off with water to which she has added apple cider vinegar, which helps remove any lingering soap.

All told she will steam for about two hours, until she begins to feel hungry. "That means you've had enough, that the banya has done its job."

"I don't stay in the banya for a long time," she says. "The banya leaves its mark on a person. It both excites, and quiets, the body. The body is in a new state."

After she dresses she will go outside, sit for "five, seven, eight minutes" before returning home by public transport. Once home "I very much like to relax in comfort. I always drink coffee. To each his own, but I like coffee. I drink two cups, not very big ones. After that I eat, but not heavily—bread and cheese, or simply some cheese." She never eats vegetables or sweets after the banya.

"Then I might nap a little bit, or I might simply lie down—a blanket pulled lightly over me. I like to stay warm, but I don't like anything weighing down on me. I don't like that. Two, three hours later I can sleep, if I want to sleep. If I don't want to sleep I watch TV, but I do so lying down."

"By evening I can already receive guests."

In winter she might have a strong drink, like vodka, but on summer evenings she will drink dry wine or a light beer. Nothing sweet.

"And that's it, my ritual—one has to have one. That's my banya day."

Mikhail's Tea

My friends and I are Sunday people at the Seleznyovsky Baths in Moscow. We only steam from ten o'clock to noon on Sunday mornings. An acquaintance, Mikhail, is a Sunday person, too, only he is usually dressing around the time we are undressing.

He shows at eight o'clock for the first two-hour steam, when the stove is hottest.

One day Mikhail lingered after he overheard me speaking English. For, in the Soviet Union, he was an expert on the United States—a so-called *Amerikanist*. He told me he simply missed speaking English, so from time to time we talk. His language skills have held up.

Mikhail works as a representative in Moscow for Tatarstan, the economically progressive, predominately Muslim republic about five hundred miles south of Russia's capital. He has been steaming regularly for more than forty years. He used to steam at the country's most famous and beautiful banya, the Sandunovsky Baths. But he left Sanduny for the superior steam at Seleznyovka.

Mikhail is a bureaucrat. He is in his early sixties, of average height and weight, with brown hair. He does not stick out. But when he begins to speak about the banya his features swell with an energy that is almost tactile. I like to sit across from him, to listen, and to watch the transformation.

"I'm waiting for this Sunday morning. I have a feeling, so to speak," he once told me, in English.

"My banya starts when I start boiling the tea at home. It means mentally I'm already in the banya. Everybody is asleep, but when I start boiling the tea—it's not usual tea, no—it's the boiling of tea, a special tea, with a number of tea types and herbs of different types, like mint, or something else, or lemon, and everything coming together.

"So I take the pot and I put the boiled water inside, but already there are three, four, five types of tea, different kinds—and green tea, and black tea, and some other. Whatever you have, you put it in there.

"Then I put it on the fire, but not too long. The moment it's starting [to boil] up you stop it, or you could lose the flavor . . . Then you take it off, you pour it through the filter, yeah, and then add some lemon, or lemon oil. Oh, no, before that, the moment it starts to boil, I usually add four or five teaspoons of preserves, whatever you have—blackberry, strawberry, whatever you have at hand. Not sugar. Sugar isn't any good whatsoever.

"Then you take it and you filter it and you put it into a thermos. And then, mentally, I'm already in the banya. It is a real banya when you bring this sort of expectation to it."

Sasha's *Veniki*

A priority for me in big-city steam rooms is the integrity of the leaves of the *veniki*, their feel on the skin, but not so much their fragrance—which is lost as it commingles with the scents of other *veniki* swirling through the same air. Sometimes I will add several drops of the extract of mint, or eucalyptus, to the water in which *veniki* are soaking; sometimes I will add the extract of valerian, which lends an especially harmonious scent to tired leaves.

Usually, though, I simply follow the recipe imparted to me by a late acquaintance from a coed banya in Moscow.

Sasha was short and gray, in his late fifties, a retired coach of the soccer team fielded by the city's police department. His smile was disarming; when he was not smiling (which was most of the time), he appeared gruff. He smoked heavily (even between steams), and it killed him.

Sasha made good steam, but his recognized skill—perhaps, even, his calling—was with *veniki*. He was a master. In fact, his abilities made him something of a ladies' man: Over the course of several hours on Wednesday evenings at the city's Varshavsky Baths, women would approach him, smiling, and ask him to massage their bodies in the steam room with the two petite bunches of supple, small-leafed oak he gathered himself in early autumn.

It can be exhausting to massage oneself, and maybe a friend.

Sasha would massage at least a half dozen people. For free.

Sasha only used oak. He cared for his *veniki* so well that, sometimes, the leafless handles would wear out faster than the leaves would fall off, and he would reinforce the bare ends by coiling them with layers of opaque packing tape.

He brought pleasure to more women in a month than most men do in a lifetime.

Sasha told me he first soaked his *veniki* in cold water for about ten minutes, then dumped out the water and refilled the basin with warm water. After soaking the *veniki* for another ten minutes, he dumped out the warm water and refilled the basin with hot water. Then he soaked the *veniki* for ten minutes more.

Only then, he told me, were *veniki* truly ready to use.

Most bathers are not patient enough to wait half an hour. Most prepare *veniki* simply by filling up basins with hot-hot water, then dipping the leafy ends anywhere from several seconds, to several minutes. Sometimes they dip the handles first, to soften them. Sometimes, too, they place a second basin on top of the first, upside down, trapping the steam while the *veniki* steep.

But only *veniki* with fresh leaves need to be soaked in hot water, alone.

In fact, *veniki* with dry leaves can be soaked entirely in cold water. One connoisseur of the banya in the city of Khabarovsk, in the Far East, told me he soaks his *veniki* overnight in cool water, then wraps them in a moist rag that he carries to the banya. He insists that leaves cared for in this manner not only hold firm, but retain their fragrance.

Still, I prefer the gradual saturation of the leaves—from cold to warm to hot. Like Sasha, I can reuse *veniki* three or four or more times (whereas, usually, *veniki* are discarded after one steam). But I cannot claim to possess the touch he exhibited once he carried his *veniki* into the steam room.

Appendix 2

Banya Sayings

«Счастливый, как из бани»
"Happy as if fresh from the banya"

«Без бани нам, как телу без души»
"Without the banya we're like a body without a soul" (Alexei Tolstoy)

«Когда бы не баня, все бы мы пропали»
"If not for the banya, we'd all be lost"

«Годы старят—баня молодит»
"The years age you, but the banya makes you younger"

«В бане парок и ладит, и гладит»
"In the banya the steam soothes you, puts you in harmony"

«Баня все грехи смоет»
"The banya washes away all sins"

«Баня всё правит»
"The banya puts everything right"

«Баня для больного всё равно, что бальзам»
"The banya is a balm for the sick"

«В тот день не старишься, который в бане паришься»
«В который день паришься—в тот день не старишься»
"You don't age the day you steam in the banya"

«Сначала—в баню, а потом—за пироги»
"First go to the banya, *then* for the pies"

«В бане веник дороже денег»
"In the banya a *venik* is worth more than money"

«В бане веник—господин»
«Веник в бане господин, или набольший»
"In the banya the *venik* is lord [and master]"

«Веник в бане всем начальник»
"In the banya a *venik* is everyone's boss"

«Веник в бане—всему голова»
"A *venik* in the banya is heads above everyone"

«Баня без веника—что самовар без трубы»
"A banya without *veniki* is like a samovar without a pipe"

«Баня без веника—что клумба без цветов»
"A banya without *veniki* is like a flower-bed without flowers"

«Баня без веника, что свадьба без невесты»!
"A banya without *veniki* is like a wedding without a bride!"

«Банный веник и царя старше»
"A *venik* is of higher order than the tsar"

«Берёзовый веник и царицу вылечил»
"A birch *venik* cured even the empress"

«Веник всех генералов перебил и царю спуску не дал»
"One *venik* thrashed all the generals, and gave no quarter to the tsar"

«В бане веник хозяин, в печи кочерга»
"In the banya the *venik* is boss, but the fire iron is boss in the stove"

«Без веника баня не парит, а пар не жарит»
"Without *veniki* the banya won't steam you, and the steam won't warm you"

«Дам баню, что до новых веников не забудешь»
"I'll give you a banya so good that you won't forget till it's time for new *veniki*"

«Баня, веник да парок—любому впрок»!
"The banya, *venik*, and steam are beneficial to everyone"

«Банный веник душу тешит да тело нежит»
"The *venik* soothes the soul and coddles the body"

«Сам с пядь, а борода до пят»
Riddle about *veniki*: "Only nine inches long, yet with a beard to the soles of its feet"

«Маленький, мохнатенький, всех людей перебил и царю не спустил»
Riddle about *veniki*: "Small, shaggy, and thrashes everyone, even the tsar"

«Дух парной, дух святой»
"The spirit of the steam room is holy"

«Дураки и после бани чешутся»
«Каких только дураков нет, некоторые и после бани чешутся»!
"Fools itch even after the banya"

«У кого бока чешутся, тот и баню ищет»
"He whose sides itch is in desperate need of the banya"

«Баня создана для тела, как песня для души»
"A banya built for the body is like a song for the soul"

«Душистый пар не только тело, но и душу лечит»
"A fragrant steam cures not only the body, but also the soul"

«Баня—храм здоровья»
"The banya is the temple of health"

«Что паришь, то и правишь»
"Whatever you steam is put right"

«Баня болезнь из тела гонит»
"The banya drives out illness from the body"

«На пару да в баньке сорок болезней выходит»
"The steam in the banya drives out forty afflictions"

«Семь потов и один недуг уходит после бани»
"Seven steams and one ailment leave after the banya"

"В бане болячка садится»
"In the banya sores disappear"

«Банный пар лечит, здоровье дарит»
«Баня полечит, здоровье подарит»
"Banya steam heals you, gifts you health"

«После доброй бани—что Ангел в чистой рани»
"A gentle steam is like an Angel appearing at the break of dawn"

«Добрая банька—лучшая нянька»
"A kind-hearted banya is the best nursemaid"

«Баня—мать родная: кости расправит, все тело поправит»
"The banya is our mother: it aligns our bones, puts right our whole body"

«Баня чистит, баня парит—баня все поправит»
"The banya cleanses, the banya steams—the banya puts everything right"

«Баня парит, баня правит, баня молодцом поставит»!
«Помыть, попарить, молодцом поставить»
"The banya steams you, the banya restores you, the banya leaves you feeling great!"

«Жаркий пар любой недуг исцелит»
"Hot steam cures any ailment"

«Баня да лук от всех недуг»
"The banya and a raw onion cure all ailments"

«Наешься луку, ступай в баню, натрись хреном, запей квасом»
"Eat a raw onion, step into the banya, rub down with horseradish root, drink *kvas*"

«Помни день субботный—иди в баню»
"Remember to go to the banya on Saturdays"

«Пару бояться—в баню не ходить»
«В баню идти, пару не боятся»
"If you're afraid of the steam, stay out of the banya"

«Пар любить, баню топить»
"To enjoy the steam, stoke the banya hot"

«Баня—здоровье семьи»
"The banya is the family's well-being"

«Постничай по средам, ходи в баню по субботам (будешь здоров)»
"Fast on Wednesdays, go to the banya on Saturdays (and you'll be healthy)"

«Баня не заговенье—на неё нет запрета»
«На баню поста нет»
"The banya isn't like fasting: it's never forbidden"

«Плохая баня всех моет, а сама вся в грязи»
"The banya washes everyone, yet itself is covered in filth"

«По дыму в бане пара не угадаешь»
"You can't tell the essence of steam from the smoke"

«Чем шелудивого брить, лучше в баньку сводить»
"Better to send someone mangy to the banya, than to shave him"

«Баня без пара, что щи без навара»
"A banya without steam is like cabbage soup without the fat"

«Москва без бань—не Москва, а баня без пара—что щи без навара»
"Moscow without banyas isn't Moscow, and a banya without steam is like cabbage soup without the fat"

«Харкая баня лучше сытного обеда»
"A hot banya is better than a filling lunch"

«Русская кость тепло любит»
"Russian bones love warmth"

«Живая кость тепло любит»
"A living bone likes warmth"

«Кости распаришь—всё тело направишь»
«В бане кости распаришь—тело поправишь»
"If you steam your bones, you'll set your whole body straight"

«Пар костей не ломит»
"Steam won't break your bones"

«Пар костей не ломит, вон души не гонит»
"Steam won't break your bones, or drive out the soul"

«В баню пришёл—должен и попотеть»
"If you've come to the banya, you need to sweat"

«Из бани, не вспотев, не выйдешь»
«Вошедший в баню, не вспотевши не выйдет»
"Don't leave the banya unless you've sweated"

«Вошёл в баню—раздевайся»
"If you're in the banya, then disrobe"

«Пропотеешь, так и жар пройдёт»
"Sweat out a fever"

«Парься—не ожгись, поддавай—не опались, с полка—не свались»
«Вот тебе баня ледяная, веники водяные, парься не ожгись, поддавай не опались, с полка не свались»
"Steam without burning yourself, add water to the stove without scorching yourself, get up from the bench without slipping"

«Душа любит прохладу, а плоть—пар»
«Душа—на прохладу, а плоть—в баню»
"The soul prefers coolness, the flesh—steam"

«Лучше быть чистым, чем сытым»
"Better to be clean, than well-fed"

«Грязь не сало, помыл—и отстала»
"Dirt isn't bacon fat, you wash it off and it leaves no residue"

«Баня дороже денег»
"The banya is worth more than money"

«И дождливый день нипочём—всё равно в баню пойдем»
"Rain or shine, we're going to the banya"

«Мойся белее, будешь милее»
"The cleaner you wash up, the sweeter you'll be"

«Чистота—лучшая красота»
"Cleanliness is the greatest beauty"

«Купи мыльце, да помой рыльце»
"Buy some soap and wash your mug [face]"

«Завтра баню собирается, так уже сегодня не умывается»
"If you're going to banya tomorrow, there's no need to wash up today"

«За паром глаз не знать»
"One can't read another's face through the steam"

«Сижу у банной печи да грею плечи»
"I sit near the stove in the banya, warm my shoulders"

«Такая парка, что небу жарко»
"A steam so hot it makes the sky swelter"

«Пятница—для стирки, суббота—для бани»
"Fridays are for laundry, Saturdays are for the banya"

«В чужой бане и пар лучше, и доски на полках глаже»
"In someone else's banya the steam is better, and the boards on the benches are smoother"

«Хороши дрова у соседа: от его бани и нам пар идёт»
"The neighbor's firewood is good: from his banya the steam makes its way to us"

«Табак да кабак, баба да баня, одна забава»
"Tobacco in the public house, a woman in the banya, it's all in good fun"

«Баня парит, баня правит»
«Кости расправить—тело поправить»
"The banya steams you, the banya restores you"

«Баня парит, баня правит, баня всё поправит»
"The banya steams, the banya rules, the banya puts everything right"

«В бане помылся—что заново родился»
«Помылся—как вновь народился»
«После парной будто вновь на свет родился»
"After steaming it's as if you've been born again"

«Поддай парок да лезь на полок»
"Make the steam, then lie down on a bench [in the steam room]"

«Сперва больше пару—меньше удару, потом все больше удару, меньше пару»
"At first make more steam, and use less force [with the *veniki*].
Then use more force [with the *veniki*], and make less steam"

«В баню ходить—не воду пить, а тело мыть»
"Go to the banya not to drink vodka, but to wash your body"

«После бани хоть портки заложи, а сто грамм выпей»
"After the banya put away your trousers, and drink one hundred grams [of vodka]"

«Париться—не стариться»
"Don't get old—steam"

«Лучше не добрать, чем перебрать»!
"It's better not to finish [steaming], than overdo it!"

Bibliography

Aaland, Mikkel. *Sweat*. Santa Barbara, CA: Capra Press, 1978.

Andreev-Khomiakov, Gennadiĭ A. *Gor'kie vody: Ocherki i rasskazy*. Frankfurt: Posev, 1954.

Applebaum, Anne. *Gulag: A History*. New York: Doubleday, 2003.

Ashenburg, Katherine. *The Dirt on Clean: An Unsanitized History*. New York: North Point Press, 2008.

Babushkin, Anatoliĭ I. *Bania: Dom zdorov'ia*. St. Petersburg: Piter, 1999.

Bani, prachechnye, i voshĕboĭka. Moscow: Tsentral'noe Voenno-Proektnoe Upravlenie, 1942.

Barakov, IUriĭ P. *Poklon russkoĭ bane*. Moscow: Russkaia Panorama, 2007.

Belousov, Pëtr P. *Sauna ili russkaia bania "Sukhoveĭ?"* Moscow: Prometei, 1991.

Bich", I. A. "Ocherk istorīi Russkoĭ bani i eia fizīologicheskoe i terapevticheskoe znachenīe." In *Pamiatnaia knizhka Grodnenskoĭ gubernīi na 1893 g.* Grodno: Tipografiia gubernskago pravleniia, 1893.

Biriukov, Anatoliĭ A. *Eto volshebnitsa bania*. Moscow: Sovetskii Sport, 1991.

———.*Priglashaem poparit'sia*. Moscow: Fizkul'tura i sport, 1987.

Blinov, Vladimir A. *Bania dlia dushi i tela*. Ekaterinburg: U-Faktoriia, 2001.

Bogdanov, Igor' A. *Tri veka Peterburgskoĭ bani*. St. Petersburg: Iskusstvo-SPb, 2000.

Borisova, M. B. *Bania vmesto lekarstva*. St. Petersburg: Ves', 2004.

Boym, Svetlana. *Common Places: Mythologies of Everyday Life in Russia*. Cambridge, MA: Harvard University Press, 1994.

Brue, Alexia. *Cathedrals of the Flesh: My Search for the Perfect Bath*. New York: Bloomsbury, 2004.

Bushkov, Ruslan A. *Bania po-Kazanski*. Kazan': Zhurnal Kazan', 1993.

Chashchin, Aleksandr. "Potomu chto est' Nikolaeva." *Pravda Severa*, 7 December 2005.

Chekhov, Anton P. *Polnoe sobranie sochineniĭ i pisem v tridtsati tomakh*. Vol. 3, *Socheneniia, 1884–1885*. Moscow: Nauka, 1975.

Chernyshev, Vladimir. *Bania: Tolkovyĭ slovar'*. Moscow: Dashkov i K., 2007.

Cross, Anthony G. "The Russian Banya in the Descriptions of Foreign Travellers and in the Depictions of Foreign and Russian Artists." *Oxford Slavonic Papers*, n.s. 24 (1991): 34–59.

Danzas, Julia N. *Bagne rouge: Souvenirs d'une prisonnière au pays des Soviets*. Juvisy: Les Éditions du Cerf, 1935.

Dostoevskiĭ, Fëdor. *Polnoe sobranie sochineniĭ*. Vol. 3, *Zapiski iz' mĕrtvaga doma*. St. Petersburg, 1892.

Dubrovin, Il'ia I. *Russkaia bania: Original'nye retsepty*. Moscow: EKSMO-Press, 2001.

Fagan, Garrett G. "Bathing for Health with Celsus and Pliny the Elder." *Classical Quarterly* 56 (2006): 190–207.

Galitskiĭ, Alekseĭ V. *Shchedryĭ zhar: Ocherki o russkoĭ bane i eë blizkikh i dal'nikh rodichakh.* Moscow: Fizkul'tura i sport, 1974.

Giliarovskiĭ, Vladimir A. *Sochineniia v chetyrëkh tomakh.* Moscow: Pravda, 1989–.

Gol'din, Igor' I. *Moskva bez ban'—ne Moskva.* Moscow: Kulturno-sportivno-ozdorovitel'nye kompleksy, 1999.

Gor'kiĭ, Maksim. "Solovki." *Nashi dostizheniia* 5 (1929).

Gromova, Galina, ed. *Skazhi mne, Gospodi, put' moĭ.* Moscow: Palomnik, 2006.

Healey, Dan. "Masculine Purity and 'Gentlemen's Mischief': Sexual Exchange and Prostitution between Russian Men, 1861–1941." *Slavic Review* 60, no. 2 (Summer 2001): 223–65.

Hellberg-Hirn, Elena. *Soil and Soul: The Symbolic World of Russianness.* Aldershot: Ashgate, 1998.

Herling, Gustaw. *A World Apart: Imprisonment in a Soviet Labor Camp during World War II.* New York: Penguin Books, 1996.

Herva, Marjatta. *Let's Have a Sauna.* Helsinki: The Finnish Sauna Society, 2002.

Hyde, Lewis. *The Gift: Creativity and the Artist in the Modern World.* New York: Vintage Books, 2007.

Johnson, Tom, and Tim Miller. *The Sauna Book.* New York: Harper & Row, 1977.

Khoshev, IUriĭ M. *Teoriia ban'.* Moscow: Kniga i Biznes, 2006.

Kon, Igor. Interview by author. Moscow, 2007.

Krinichnaia, Neonila A., IAkov R. Rybkin, Vladimir I. Antokhin, Tat'iana V. Antokhina, Ėdvin P. Alatalo, and Anatoliĭ S. Onegov. *Bania, ban'ka, baenka: Liubiteliam i znatokam bannogo dela.* Petrozavodsk: Kareliia, 1992.

Likhachev, Dmitriĭ S. *Arkhitekturno-khudozhestvennye pamiatniki Solovetskikh ostrovov.* Moscow: Iskusstvo, 1980.

———. *Vospominaniia.* St. Petersburg: Logos, 1995.

Lipinskaia, Viktoriia A., Liudmila N. Chizhikova, Tat'iana S. Makashina, Igor' A. Morozov, Andreĭ A. Zheltov, and Igor' I. Gol'din. *Bania i pech' v Russkoĭ narodnoĭ traditsii.* Moscow: Intrada, 2004.

Litavar, Viacheslav V., and Gennadiĭ L. Kaĭdanov. *Kak postroit' pech', kamin, baniu.* Minsk: Uradzhai, 1990

Lloyd Parry, Richard. "Long-Lost Soldier, 83, Returns To Ukraine." *The Times of London*, 21 April 2006.

———. "Mr. Uwano Comes Back from the Dead to Say 'Good Day.'" *The Times of London*, 20 April 2006.

Lopatin, Ivan A. "Origin of the Native American Steam Bath." *American Anthropologist*, n.s. 62, no. 6 (December 1960): 977–93.

Martirosian, K. G. "Russkaia literatura 19 veka (vtoraia polovina)." Introductory Lecture, undated. <http://rudocs.exdat.com/docs/index-386551.html?page=5>.

Matveev, P. N. "Sanitarnyĭ minimum v obshchestvennykh baniakh." PhD diss., MEDGIZ, 1932.

McLellan, Josie. "State Socialist Bodies: East German Nudism from Ban to Boom." *The Journal of Modern History* 79, no. 1 (March 2007): 48–79.

Mogil'nyĭ, Nikolaĭ P. *Russkaia bania*. Moscow: TERRA-Knizhnyi Klub, 2001.

Nikonova, Liudmila I., and Irina A. Kandrina. *Bania v sisteme zhizneobespecheniia narodov Povolzh'ia i Priural'ia*. Saransk: Izd-vo Mordovskogo universiteta, 2003.

———. *Kak lechilis' narody Povolzh'ia i Priural'ia*. Saransk, Russia: NII gumanitarnykh nauk pri Pravitel'stve Respubliki Mordoviia, 2005.

Nurmakhanov, A. "O vliianii peregrevaniia v usloviiakh parnoĭ bani na funktsional'noe sostoianie organizma." PhD diss., S. M. Kirov State University, 1972.

Passek, Vadim. *Ocherki Rossīi*. St. Petersburg: N. Grech, 1838.

Pollock, Ethan. "'Real Men Go to the Bania': Postwar Soviet Masculinities and the Bathhouse." *Kritika: Explorations in Russian and Eurasian History* 11, no. 1 (Winter 2010): 47–76.

Pushkin, Aleksandr. *Eugene Onegin: A Novel in Verse*. Trans. James E. Falen. New York: Oxford University Press, 1995.

———. *Evgeniĭ Onegin*. St. Petersburg, 1837.

Robson, Roy R. *Solovki: The Story of Russia Told Through Its Most Remarkable Islands*. New Haven, CT: Yale University Press, 2004.

Rubinov, Anatoliĭ Z. *Istoriia Bani*. Moscow: Novoe literaturnoe obozrenie, 2006.

———. *Sanduny: Kniga o moskovskikh baniakh*. Moscow: Moskovskii rabochii, 1990.

Ryan, William F. *The Bathhouse at Midnight: An Historical Survey of Magic and Divination in Russia*. University Park: Pennsylvania State University Press, 1999.

Sanches, Antonio Nunes Ribeiro. *O parnykh rossiĭskikh baniakh: Poeliku spospeshestvuiut one ukrepleniiu, sokhraneniiu i vozstanovleniiu zdraviia*. St. Petersburg, 1779.

Sauna Studies: Papers Read at the VI International Sauna Congress in Helsinki on August 15–17, 1974. Helsinki: The Finnish Sauna Society, 1976.

Scott, John. *Behind the Urals: An American Worker in Russia's City of Steel*. Bloomington: Indiana University Press, 1973.

Shalamov, Varlam T. *Sobranie sochineniĭ*. Vol. 1. Moscow: Khudozhestvennaia literatura, 1998.

Shukshin, Vasiliĭ M. *Rasskazy, Povesti, 1925–1974*. Moscow: Drofa, 2002.

Solzhenitsyn, Aleksandr I. *The Gulag Archipelago 1918–1956: An Experiment in Literary Investigation*. New York: Harper & Row, 1974.

Tallemant des Réaux, Gédéon. *Les Historiettes*. Vol. 1. Trans. Hamish Miles. New York: Brentano, 1920.

Tolstoĭ, Lev. *Voĭna i mir*. Vol. 2. Khar'kov: PARUS, 2014.

Vigarello, Georges. *Concepts of Cleanliness: Changing Attitudes in France since the Middle Ages*. Trans. Jean Birrell. Cambridge: Cambridge University Press, 1988.

Volkov, Oleg V. *Pogruzhenie vo t'mu.* Belaia kniga Rossii 4. Moscow: Molodaia gvardiia, 1989.

Williams, Marilyn T. *Washing "The Great Unwashed": Public Baths in Urban America, 1840–1920.* Columbus: Ohio State University Press, 1991.

Zheltov, Andreĭ A. "Russkaia bania i starinnyĭ severnyĭ byt." *Ėtnograficheskoe obozrenie,* no. 3 (1999): 35–51.

Znamenskiĭ, Vissarion. "O Russkikh baniakh' v" gigīenicheskom" otnoshenīi." PhD diss., Sankt-Peterburgskoĭ bol'nitsy chërnorabochikh, 1861.

Zoshchenko, Mikhail M. *Scenes from the Bathhouse and Other Stories of Communist Russia.* Ann Arbor: The University of Michigan Press, 1961.

———. *Rasskazy.* Smolensk: Rusich, 1997.

Acknowledgments

There is no such thing as a self-made man, and there is no such thing as a self-made book. I don't know all the ways people conspired to help me on my way, but I know this: The idea for the book almost surely wouldn't have come to me if not for Grigory Aleksandrovich Konkin, who makes the best steam in Moscow, and taught me how to do it. Grisha allowed me into an otherwise closed world from which I could see myself, and Russia, with different eyes. Through him, moreover, my working knowledge of *nenormativnaya leksika* (foul language) soared to uncommon heights!

There were others who opened up doors for me, and to whom I am especially grateful: John Freedman, Nataliya Comizzoli, and Viktor Nutnikov in Moscow; Sergei Puskepalis in Magnitogorsk; Gennady and Maria Tabakov in Chuvashiya; and Father Gerasim on the Solovki.

During an interview the late Igor Kon told me—to my great shock—that "a book isn't written only once." As in so many other respects, he was right.

To that end, I am particularly grateful to my first readers: Frank Brown, Erika MacWilliams, and Cathy Lord. My former Russian literature professor, Murl Barker—who led a college trip to the Soviet Union, and (wittingly?) helped shape the *sud'ba* (fate) that took me again to that part of the world—gave my draft manuscript a meticulous read. Others, too, helped with valuable feedback: Peter Murphy, Roy Robson, Steve Myers, David Wheeler, Ron Miller, Francis Collins, Diane MacWilliams, Bruce MacWilliams, and Patty Enright.

Minna Proctor published an excerpt of the chapter, "The Banya Is Holy," in an issue of *The Literary Review* that sent me scrambling to find yet more work from the eye-opening poets and writers she also included. Kathleen Volk Miller, coeditor of *Painted Bride Quarterly*, invited me to curate a reading that highlighted fragments from the book.

Translating Russian from different centuries presents challenges, especially for someone who first began to study the language following the Soviet collapse. I tried to be sparing with my questions, and spread around the pain, notably to: Svetlana Krakopolskaya, Ben Hooson, Liya Grishaeva, Maria Danek, Ilya Utekhin, Maria Golubeva, Murl Barker, and John Freedman.

For a time Ellen Anastos provided me with space to live, and write, atop a mountain in Cyprus. Eric Wenberg and Pamela Quanrud provided me with space in Warsaw. Isabel DeSousa did so in Lisbon, and Kari Ahlberg did in Helsinki. My mom, Diane MacWilliams, gave me an upstairs bedroom in South Jersey from which I pledge to clear out boxes . . . soon.

Peter Murphy said yes when I needed to have a conversation with someone other than myself. Little did I know he was the godfather of a community of writers (mostly poets, no less!) that has emerged as a crucial touchstone of support and friendship.

Laura Engelstein, Roy Robson, Dan Healey, Ethan Pollock, and Sibelan Forrester fielded stray questions I needed the help of true Russia scholars to answer.

Amy Farranto, my editor at Northern Illinois University Press, shepherded my manuscript—and me—through the publication process with a practiced, yet intuitive, hand.

The staff in Reading Hall No. 1 at the Russian State Library, or "Leninka," welcomed me in the mornings for months, and held books for me without flouting the rules . . . too much. In the States I didn't have access to a vast library collection or interlibrary loan service, but David Azzolina at Charles Patterson Van Pelt Library at the University of Pennsylvania helped me chase down, and read, English-language sources. Staff at the Slavic Reference Service at the University of Illinois found high-resolution images of banya-related art when I couldn't.

Early drafts were written, in part, at my ad hoc offices in Moscow—the Coffee Beans on Pyatnitskaya and Pokrovka Streets. In the States revisions were made at: the Yale University Divinity School Library; the Mullica Hill Branch of the Gloucester County Library System; and Grooveground coffee bar in Collingswood, New Jersey. No one ever told me that I'd overstayed my welcome, but I'm sure I came close.

James Hill broke an unintentional sweat when he brought his

two-and-a-quarter to Seleznyovka on a sanitary day, then generously allowed me to share his photographs with readers.

The late Lucille DeView, writing coach at my last full-time newspaper gig, pushed me to pursue more than journalism prizes with my writing. I might not have pursued journalism, at all, if my high school literature teacher, John Howard, hadn't mentioned to a relative that he thought I could write. And everything I needed to know about English grammar I learned from Mrs. Shirley Myers in fifth and sixth grade. I cling to what she taught me with torn fingernails.

Finally, grateful acknowledgment is due to the following publishers and individuals who granted me permission to translate and otherwise reprint materials for my book: Mikkel Aaland; Cambridge University Press; Göttingen State and University Library; HarperCollins Publishers; Karin Hartmann and Tony Hendrik; James Hill; Indiana University Press; Intrada; Freddy Jaklitsch and Andy Schweitzer; Neonila A. Krinichnaya; Oxford University Press; Papageno, Vienna; Penn State University Press; Posev; Vladimir F. Shishinin; The Times of London; Wellcome Library, London; and Yale University Press.